Blessings,
Dr. C. Philip Chacko

"I have thoroughly enjoyed *Online with God*. I often read a book with the leading question: 'Does this leave me thinking in new ways?' The simple answer is, yes, it does! It offers a succinct description of spirit and soul, mind, and body, and the relationship of these to the triangle of the Holy Trinity. It is refreshing and renewing to read. I will follow the forty days and read them again, one day at a time!

"[Dr. Chacko's] book offers nothing less than a truly holistic view of the human condition. It moves us from brokenness experienced as disharmony among our natural internal dialogue partners to a clear understanding of healing, harmony, and full spiritual union with Self-God-Other. I closed the book saying to myself, 'I also want this kind of internal harmony so that I can be a person who creatively changes the world (through my words and my actions).'"

—REV. DR. TAMARA NICHOLS RODENBERG
President of Bethany College

"Rarely does one bask in an illumination of complex matters that sparks a person to act and think in a whole new way about God, the world, human life, and the intricate relationships among them all. Dr. Philip Chacko has delivered such a description of the character of God—'the Trinity' or 'Triangle' of relations—of One Being as Father, Son, and Holy Spirit, whose form of Life becomes constitutive of the image that every human embodies."

—DR. DAVID P. MOESSNER
Chair of Religion at Texas Christian University

"*Online with God* is a delightful blend of scholarly thought and practical instruction. While the first two chapters describe the nuts and bolts of the triangle theory, the book slowly evolves into familiar examples that showcase the relatability of the theory. I especially like the last two chapters with the exercises and spiritual disciplines, where [Dr. Chacko] show[s] us how to get started on a balanced life."

—JUDY PHARISS COLLINS
Manager of Pastoral Care at Texas Health Kaufman

"Dr. Chacko is a man of faith as he radiates God's light and love to all who know him. Through his teachings, he brings each of us closer to understanding the power of our living Lord. *Online with God* allows us to realize the connectivity we can experience by keeping God as the center of our lives. Dr. Chacko reminds us of the discipline needed to be in harmony, so we can be led by God to do his will and in return receive the fullness that only God can give. Your life can be changed if you embrace the triangle theory!"

—PYLAR PINKSTON
First Vice President and Senior
Investment Manager of Wells Fargo Advisors

"Theologically brilliant and astute . . . I highly recommend this persuasive biblical and scholarly treatment on the work of the triune God in the world. It is written with passion, in a reader-friendly style with well-crafted words and powerful illustrations . . . The book with its provocative insights, is a special gift of God for us all!"

—DR. SAPHIR ATHYAL
Director of Faith & Development at World Vision International,
Founder-Chairman of Asia Theological Association,
and Former Principal of Union Biblical Seminary

ONLINE WITH GOD

ONLINE WITH GOD

A Triangle Theory for Personal

Empowerment and Biblical Understanding

Dr. C. Philip Chacko

BROWN
CHRISTIAN PRESS
A DIVISION OF
BROWN BOOKS PUBLISHING

Online with God
A Triangle Theory for Personal Empowerment and Biblical Understanding

Brown Christian Press
Dallas / New York
www.BrownChristianPress.com
(972) 381-0009

A New Era in Publishing®

Publisher's Cataloging-In-Publication Data

Names: Chacko, C. Philip, author.
Title: Online with God : a triangle theory for personal empowerment and Biblical understanding
   / Dr. C. Philip Chacko.
Description: Dallas ; New York : Brown Christian Press, a division of Brown Books Publishing,
   [2021]
Identifiers: ISBN 9781612545240
Subjects: LCSH: God--Worship and love--Biblical teaching. | Self-actualization (Psychology)--
   Religious aspects--Christianity. | Self-confidence--Religious aspects--Christianity.
Classification: LCC BV4501.3 .C43 2021 | DDC 248.4--dc23

ISBN 978-1-61254-524-0
LCCN 2021903176

Printed in the United States
10 9 8 7 6 5 4 3 2 1

For more information or to contact the author, please go to
www.OnlineWithGod.com.

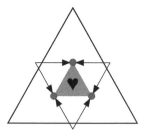

I dedicate this book to the professors and administration of Brite Divinity School, who prepared me for the Christian ministry and helped me open my eyes to see and my ears to hear God's words clearly. Most of these outstanding professors have gone to their eternal homes, but their teachings remain alive in me. They are the late Dr. Hunter Beckelhymer, Dr. Glenn Routt, Dr. Charles Kemp, and Dr. Marcus Bryant. Those who are retired and still among us are Dr. Gilbert Davis, Dr. Walter Naff, and Dr. J. Cy Rowell.

Over the last forty-five years, the faculty and administration of Brite Divinity School have enriched my professional life. Rev. Dr. Tamara Nichols Rodenberg, then vice president of Brite and now president of Bethany College in West Virginia, read the first draft of *Online with God*. Her positive and encouraging review gave me the needed incentive to put the book together for publication. Dr. D. Newell Williams, president of Brite, is also a longtime friend who kept me connected with the school in many ways.

Furthermore, I dedicate this book for the glory of God to a school where I experienced the human touch of the Divine.

Shoot for the moon. Even if you miss, you'll land among the stars.

NORMAN VINCENT PEALE

CONTENTS

FOREWORD   xiii

PREFACE   xv

ACKNOWLEDGMENTS   xvii

INTRODUCTION   1

1   THE TRIANGLE THEORY   5

2   GOD AS A TRIANGLE   29

3   THE ACCOUNT OF ADAM AND EVE   45

4   UNDERSTANDING THE BIBLE   69

5   APPLICATIONS OF THE BASIC WORKING TRIANGLE   81

6   DISCIPLINE TO ACTUALIZE THE FULLNESS OF LIFE   99

7   CREATING A NEW WORLD   111

8   LIVING IN THE NEW WORLD   137

9   REMOVING INHIBITIONS AND FRICTIONS   151

10   FULFILLING YOUR PURPOSE AND ENJOYING THE FULLNESS OF LIFE   171

11   PRACTICE THE DISCIPLINE   185

12   FORTY DAILY DEVOTIONALS   191

GLOSSARY   233

NOTES   237

BIBLIOGRAPHY   239

ABOUT THE AUTHOR   241

FOREWORD

I have observed Philip Chacko's ministry for over forty years. An immigrant from India to the United States, he was the pastor of a thriving congregation in Fort Worth, Texas, when first we met. I remember his amazing energy, joyful demeanor, and patient and kind interactions with others. Later, when he served not one congregation but many as Area Minister to East Texas for the Christian Church (Disciples of Christ), I observed the integrity, grace, and effectiveness that marked his support and oversight of several Hispanic, African American, and Anglo communities. Most recently, I have observed his ministry to a congregation that grew in its caring outreach to the larger world through his faithful and loving leadership.

How does one become the kind of centered, joyful, dynamic, and community- and life-changing person that I have known in Philip Chacko? In this book, Philip shares his understanding of humans and how God, the source of creative energy, desires to work in us to help us fulfill our human potential for love and relationships. He shows how our new internal world enables us to create a new external world. Drawing upon Scripture and his rich understanding of the human experience, Philip offers the practice of spiritual disciplines to get us started and to enrich our journeys toward becoming people who, out of their enjoyment of the fullness of life, help to make a better world.

Philip calls us to believe that we can be the "salt of the earth and light of the world." I encourage you to read the pages that follow as a gift from one who knows firsthand that opening ourselves to God's creative energy can bring purpose, joy, and satisfaction to our lives as fully-actualized human beings.

D. Newell Williams

President and Professor of Modern and American Church History

Brite Divinity School

Texas Christian University

Preface

I found myself often confessing with the Apostle Paul: "I do not understand my own actions. For I do not do what I want, but I do the very thing I hate" (Romans 7:15). My search for answers to find harmony in human nature led me to what I call the "triangle theory." This theory states that God is a triangle, comprised of Father, Son, and Holy Spirit. God created human beings in His image with four triangles:

1. Body, Soul, and Spirit
2. Reason, Emotion, and Morals
3. Thought, Desire, and Will
4. Conscious Mind, Subconscious Mind, and Unconscious Mind

The interaction of these triangles makes a human being. However, our triangles are like siblings in a family who do not always get along with one another, and they cause disharmony within the inner being. They can be balanced only by a higher power.

In most of us, one member of a triangle family—such as desire—often takes control over the other members and forces them to follow. That dominant member convinces all the other members of the body that they will suffer if this one member is not appeased. Therefore, we find ourselves enslaved to the body's needs and desires.

God's triangle (Father, Son, and Holy Spirit) is the only power that can keep all human triangles in harmony. The teaching of Jesus—"Strive first for the kingdom of God and his righteousness, and all these things will be given to you as well"—is the truth (Matthew 6:33)! In *Online with God*, you will discover how to overcome the resistance of your four triangles and instead give control to God, enjoy the richness of life on earth, and live with the hope of life everlasting.

Acknowledgments

Online with God is the result of a lifetime journey. My story begins with my parents, who instilled within my siblings and me the importance of faith. I was further guided by my Sunday school teachers and Christian friends who spiritually supported my parents and me. They were God's visible reality and helped me establish a foundation in the Christian faith.

Even after I fully surrendered my life to the path of the cross, I often failed to balance my inner being. God blessed me with a companion who stood by my side for over fifty years and helped balance my emotional roller coaster. I am much obliged to my wife, Elizabeth, for helping me become who I am through the many challenges and changes in life. Our middle son, Stephen, quietly watched me formulate the triangle theory, always seeking the best in me, and our older son, Vincent, and his wife, Amber, encouraged me to practice the theory before I shared it with others. Our daughter, Sarah Beth, helped me find the words to explain it. Their love for me and my faith in God during the hardest time of my life as I was diagnosed with COVID-19 resulted in amazing discoveries that led to the practical reality of the triangle theory. I am deeply thankful to my family for their contribution in helping me write this book. The many parishioners and pastors whom I served as a pastor and Northeast Texas area minister helped me to teach the triangle theory and learn from it as well.

Finally, I would like to say a word of appreciation to Milli Brown, CEO of Brown Books Publishing Group, for her enthusiastic acceptance of *Online with God* and patient work with me to get it published. Her staff, particularly Samantha Williams and editors Hallie Raymond and Katherine McClellan, were a great help in shaping the manuscript into a book.

I thank God for giving me both the insight into the triangle theory and the strength to help me practice it. As I followed this theory as a spiritual discipline, God granted me everything I wished for in this earthly life more abundantly than I imagined. Practicing the triangle theory, I enjoy living each day, and I look forward to spending eternity in the presence of my loving God.

Introduction

During the last one hundred years, we have discovered the possibilities of fast movement. Motorized vehicles replaced slow-moving, animal-drawn carriages. Large metal ships, like floating cities, replaced wooden sailboats. Supersonic aircraft removed the unthinkable distance of faraway places. Today, people can travel across the globe within hours. We no longer depend on daylight for travel or business, as did the people of long ago. We talk to people in different parts of the world as if they are next door. In other words, the vast and wild world of ages past is now brought together as a global village.

In this global village, our technologies shape our lifestyle in a way in which every fraction of a second is valuable. This is evident not only within the high-tech industries but also in our everyday lives. Most people do not bother with currency and instead make their transactions with plastic cards or apps on their cell phones. Invisible digital technology can process information globally within seconds. We can write volumes about the changes in science and technology. Human discoveries are not complete, and the future generations may judge ours as slow-paced, just as the present generation looks at the past generations. Humankind has unlimited and amazing potential and possibilities ahead of them.

Progress brings change, and change is not easily understood, adapted, or accepted. In every generation—from the Stone Age to the wireless age—we face critics. When a man in Galilee talked about God in a way that did not conform to the popular norms of the religion at the time, they killed him. Galileo, Copernicus, and other forerunners of truthful discoveries could not change the minds of their critics. These men applied their minds beyond popular beliefs to understand the universe in which they lived. Their persecutors—the religious leaders of their world—were afraid of change, so they killed them as enemies of God.

When we look at world religions, considerable misinformation misleads people, causing war and strife. Religious beliefs and practices often divide people and pit them against each other. Fights between religious groups have lasted centuries. People commit unthinkable atrocities unto their fellow human beings, all in the name of God. There should be a better and more wholesome way to practice religion.

A critical look at Christianity helps us to recognize that, as a religion, it is divided against its teaching of unity and love. When people stand divided, each group is determined to protect their own interests. One must ask this question: are any of these groups a visible manifestation of the kingdom of God for which Jesus advocated?

A careful examination shows that, on the one hand, each group has some beliefs and practices that make them different from others. On the other hand, these differences do not change the fact that we must build a wholesome society as the kingdom of God. Christians are followers of Christ. They are called to make a positive difference in the world as the salt of the earth and the light of the world. But are Christians progressing and influencing the world at the rate of science and technology?

Most Americans profess a church membership, and at least thirty-five percent of them claim to be "born again" Christians. Thirty-five percent makes a lot of difference. Thirty-five percent salt makes food exceedingly salty! The truth is that most churches are more interested in attracting more members to their church communities than they are in bringing those people to the kingdom of God. Often, church leadership likes to have people of their own race, color, and socio-economic conditions.

Many ministers who have built megachurches with thousands of congregants and sought to project the image of the kingdom of God became victims of passion and pride. This does not only happen to acclaimed preachers and evangelists but also to pastors of small and large churches who often fail to live out the standards to which they have committed. The revelations of sexual misconducts within the clergy are a painful reality. People who commit their lives to Christ with good intentions to follow Jesus often fail to keep their commitments.

A radical change in understanding the Bible and its practices must take place to make Christianity a practical religion. Religious affirmation, church membership, worship, and other practices are important in human society. However, Christianity must remove fears that limit a person's rightful relationship with God. It should help us fulfill the human potential invested in each one of us by the Creator. Christianity should make such a positive difference in one's personal life and relationships that it impacts the world at large.

Although what I teach in this book is based on the Bible and the teachings of Jesus, its application is universal for all human beings. We are all created equal with fundamental foundations. *Online with God* explores the intricate foundations of humanity and how they act upon and interact with one another. It leads us from the theoretical and into the practical ways to live and enjoy living in the world.

I attempt to explain the Bible in nontraditional ways as a practical spiritual discipline and the teachings of Jesus Christ as a proactive formula for life, realizing the vision of the prophet who proclaimed, "The days are surely coming, says the Lord, when I will make a new covenant with the house of Israel and the house of Judah . . . I will put my law within them, and I will write it on their hearts; and I will be their God, and they shall be my people" (Jeremiah 31:31, 33; Hebrews 8:8, 10).

Jesus simplified this when he said, "On that day you will know that I am in my Father, and you in me, and I in you" (John 14:20). As you start reading this book, also start reading the daily devotions found in the final chapter. The study questions at the end of every chapter will reinforce your understanding of the material, and the daily devotions will lead you in the practice of spiritual discipline. We are called to connect our inner beings with the ultimate source of creation and experience the presence and power of God. This is being online with God.

CHAPTER

1

THE TRIANGLE THEORY

The Bible teaches that God is the source of all beginning. But who is God? God is a triangle made up of the Father, Son, and Holy Spirit. The Bible says that God created human beings in His image. Who—or what—is a human being?

The nature of human beings can be divided into four triangles:

1. Body, Soul, and Spirit
2. Reason, Emotion, and Morals
3. Thought, Desire, and Will
4. Conscious Mind, Subconscious Mind, and Unconscious Mind

The interactions of the members of these four triangles comprise a human being. The members of the triangles are like the siblings of a family. Sometimes they work together, and other times they only work with select members of the family. When the members of the four triangles do not work together, the inner being experiences tension and fragmentation.

We are creatures of the natural world. God, the Creator, granted us the ability to transcend our spirits beyond the natural world and interact with God's Spirit.

God is the creative energy, that which is good, divine, constructive, and holy. This creative energy is the manifestation of the Father, Son, and Holy Spirit in Christian theology. Living in fellowship with God is living in harmony with one's inner being and with God's Spirit. Growing in fellowship with God means to participate in God's creative energy, which allows us to experience tranquility in our inner being, overcome existential anxieties, and enjoy the fullness of life. In this peaceful state, the members of each triangle are guided by God's Spirit to interact with one another in harmony. When all members of the four triangles act in agreement with one another, they participate in the source of creative energy. This harmonious interaction produces peace and the fulfillment of our human potential.

FIRST TRIANGLE: BODY, SOUL, AND SPIRIT

HUMAN BODY

The body is made of flesh, blood, bones, organs, tissues, and cells. It is the physical structure of a person, made of natural substances. Therefore, it needs natural substances for growth and survival.

"The adult body as a whole is made up of 65 percent oxygen, 18 percent carbon, 10 percent hydrogen, 3 percent nitrogen, 1.5 percent calcium, 1 percent phosphorus, and 1.5 percent of other elements. About seven-tenths of the body is water. The major systems of the body include; (1) the skeletal-muscular system, (2) the digestive system, (3) the urinary system, (4) the respiratory system, (5) the circulatory system, (6) the nervous system, (7) the reproductive system."[1]

Each system has its specific task, but no system can work unless it is connected to the whole. These interdependent systems comprise the total body, which is the essence of our earthly existence.

The cell is the basic unit of the body. Each cell contains water, proteins, fats, sugars, and starch. Cells cannot function and grow without the basic materials that support them: air, water, and food. Cellular growth is important for the body's survival. Cells require a variety of foods to function and maintain and grow the human body. Different types of cells connect to make tissues, tissues connect to make organs, and organs come together in systems that function to keep the body alive.

"Inside, my stomach, spleen, liver, pancreas, and kidneys, each packed with millions of loyal cells, are working so efficiently I have no way of perceiving their presence. Fine hairs in my inner ear are monitoring a swishing fluid, ready to alert me if I suddenly tilt off balance."[2]

The body is concerned with survival and growth. It generates hunger and thirst, and then seeks food and drink. Though the tongue appears to satisfy hunger and cravings, according to science, it is the brain that generates, controls, and registers the body's satisfied state. Hunger for different kinds of food and drink is also associated with the brain per the body's needs. The body can consume food and drink beyond the essential need for survival and growth, which can work against the wellness of the body.

HUMAN SOUL

The soul provides the energy that makes the body function as a living organism. According to the Hebrew Bible, the soul comes directly from God: "Then the Lord God formed man from the dust of the ground, and breathed into his nostrils the breath of life; and the man became a living being" (Genesis 2:7).

The soul is the intricate and invisible force that gives life to the body. "In the [Old Testament] it never means the immortal soul, but it is essentially the life principle, or the living being, or the self as the subject of appetite, and emotion, occasionally of volition."[3]

In many Hebrew texts, the life principle is linked by blood. The soul exists in the blood as a material basis for life. The words *heart*, *soul*, and *spirit* are often used synonymously.

In Christian theology, the terms *soul* and *spirit* are also used synonymously. Christian theology teaches that the soul is eternal and immortal; therefore, saving the soul is required for eternal life. When it is not saved, it will be damned forever.

The mystery of the soul is not easily understood. Many books and articles have been written about the soul. Most of them are associated with religion. From primitive time to the present day, religious people have believed the soul is the essence of life. Most religions teach that the soul is eternal.

The soul is not an organic substance like the body, but it gives life to that natural substance. However, the body cannot create the soul or force it to live in the body. Therefore, the soul is supernatural and can be influenced positively or negatively.

"The evidence from decades of scientific experiments that indicate all-natural phenomena (atoms, molecules, energy, and forces) interact according to laws; and the evidence that humans have free will . . . Thus, free will cannot be explained as a natural phenomenon that is subject to laws. By definition, a phenomenon that is not subject to the laws of nature is referred to as a supernatural phenomenon. This supernatural phenomenon which is the source of free will is generally known as a 'Soul.'"[4]

HUMAN SPIRIT

The spirit is energy that remains in the body and mind as the essence of all actions. The human spirit can transcend the mind beyond the body and reach God's Spirit, enjoying fellowship with God and other humans. There is no clear definition of the human spirit in the Hebrew Bible or in the New Testament. The spirit is often associated with a ghost, such as the spirit of a dead person that visits the living.

Modern writers do not give a clear distinction between soul and spirit, but the Hebrew Bible and the New Testament offer a subtle difference between the two. According to the Hebrew Bible, at the beginning of creation, the Spirit of God was blowing, hovering, or sweeping over the dark, chaotic, and formless void. It is the Spirit of God who brought order out of the chaos. In the act of human creation, it was not a wind, but the personal breath of God that brought life to the first human being. The breath of God contained not only the life-giving soul, but also the transcendental power of God's Spirit. The Spirit of God is faster than the fastest internet. The spirit can bring into the mind thoughts of people of faraway places and the invisible God within a fraction of a second.

Even though most writers do not give a clear distinction between the soul and spirit, there is a clear distinction. The soul is that which gives life. Without an active soul, the body dies. We can live and breathe for a long time in a vegetative or comatose state. However, in this state, our spirits are not active. In the vegetative state, the soul is active, but the spirit is dormant. In this type of dormant state, the spirit does not leave the body. It remains, though it does not process information or interact with other members of the triangles. The spirit is an independent member of the first triangle that works with all members of the other triangles.

"In the models of Daniel A. Helminiak and Bernard Lonergan, human spirit is considered to be the mental functions of awareness, insight, understanding, judgement and other reasoning powers. It is distinguished from the separate component of psyche which comprises the entities of emotion, images, memory and personality."[5]

The spirit is embedded in the soul; when the soul leaves the body, the spirit also departs. While the spirit is in the active state, both the soul and spirit interact with each other and with the other triangles. The spirit has transcendental ability. It can imagine and process thoughts, interact with the members of the triangles, and have fellowship with others and with the Spirit of the Creator.

In the Hebrew Bible, God's Spirit inspired the prophets to speak God's message. The Hebrew fathers and mothers of faith heard God and understood His will for their lives. Whether they heard external voices or received internal spiritual guidance is not always clear. What is clear is that they followed God's directions. This is evident in the accounts of Noah, Abraham, Moses, Joshua, Deborah, and other leaders.

In the New Testament, Jesus followed the will of God. We read a few references of God's external voice, heard by Jesus and His disciples, but Jesus mostly received internal guidance from the Spirit of God. This is referred to as God's Spirit interacting with His followers' spirits: "And I will ask the Father, and he will give you another advocate . . . to be with you forever—the Spirit of truth. The world cannot accept him, because it neither sees him nor knows him. But you know him, for he lives with you and will be in you" (John 14:16–17, NIV).

In Jesus's encounter with Nicodemus, a Jewish rabbi, Jesus told him that he should be born again. Nicodemus asked how that could be possible. "Jesus answered, 'Very truly, I tell you, no one can enter the kingdom of God without being born of water and Spirit. What is born of the flesh is flesh, and what is born of the Spirit is spirit. Do not be astonished that I said to you, "You must be born from above." The wind blows where it chooses, and you hear the sound of it, but you do not know where it comes from or where it goes. So it is with everyone who is born of the Spirit'" (John 3:5–8).

In Christian theology, a person must be born again by the Spirit of God to commune with God's Spirit and inherit eternal life. When a person is not born again by the Spirit of God, he is not able to commune with God or inherit eternal life. It appears that both the soul and the spirit depart the body for either eternal life or eternal death. Eternal life means being with God forever, while eternal death means separation from God forever.

SECOND TRIANGLE: REASON, EMOTION, AND MORALS

The second triangle is reason, emotion, and morals. These members are the most active workforce in human personality. Therefore, they can be classified as the "basic working triangle." They act like siblings of one family. Every action a person makes can be attributed to the members of this triangle.

REASON

Reason is based on fact. We can recognize facts. Facts are knowledge. Knowledge is learned and experienced. Knowledge is stored in the brain, and the brain is greater than a computer full of data files and microchips. The brain has storage space where knowledge is deposited. Learned knowledge can be found in one file, and experienced knowledge can be found in another. Knowledge interacts with incoming information from the external world, such as the use of tools and technology, the taste of foods and drinks, educational theories, experiments of theories and their results, and more. Knowledge grows with new ideas and experiences, accumulating these things as facts. Facts guide our rational abilities to act based on the information in the brain. Facts interact with other facts to create new possibilities.

Reason interacts with the members of the other triangles. It associates with thought; thought acts like a close cousin in this triangle family. Together, they process information, which is called "reasoning." Information from other members of the triangle family also influences the process of reasoning. Reasoning processes information as reflective thinking, which can be inductive or deductive.

Inductive reasoning is based on available facts but is inconclusive. For example, when a person sees a wildfire, they may conclude that someone started the fire, but they cannot be sure whether the fire was caused by humans or lightning. They cannot make a firm conclusion about a probable cause. However, deductive reasoning is conclusive. If one sees a person setting fire to the forest, they then view the forest as on fire due to human action.

"Reasoning can be inductive or deductive. People use *inductive reasoning* when they see a puddle of water and infer that it has rained recently. Inductive reasoning is not conclusive. The evidence only makes the conclusion probable. People use *deductive reasoning* when they assert that, if life requires oxygen, then where there is life there must be oxygen. Deductive reasoning shows that must be true if the evidence is valid."[6]

Reflective thinking is when we process information for action. It can change one's established beliefs and conclusions based on new facts. Reflective thinking is also known as critical thinking. The generations who believed that the earth was flat based their beliefs on the evidence they had. Receiving new information based on new knowledge about the universe is called reflective thinking, which brought new understanding about the universe. New understanding changes already-established beliefs. It can be challenging—even threatening—or it can be liberating, opening doors for new possibilities.

EMOTION

The English word *emotion* is derived from the French word *émouvoir*, meaning to agitate or stir up. This is based on the Latin word *emovere*, for "move." *Webster's New World Dictionary* defines emotion as "1. a) Strong feeling; excitement; b) the state or capacity of having the feelings aroused to the point of awareness; 2. any specific feelings: any of various complex reactions with both mental and physical manifestations, as love, hate fear, anger, etc."[7]

Emotion is a strong member of the second triangle. It generates feelings for our protection, provision, and enjoyment. Feelings are essential for the wellbeing of the entire human body and all the members of the triangles of the inner beings.

Emotion is a process of feelings-based response. When the body faces harm, emotion (often quickly) responds and defends the body through physical and verbal actions, both externally and internally. Emotions are classified as good and bad, positive and negative.

We often attribute feelings like love, peace, joy, thanksgiving, acceptance, adorations, gentleness, kindness, courage, excitement, and enthusiasm as good emotions. We also see bad emotions, such as hate, anger, fear, indifference, arrogance, rudeness, apathy, and unconcern. However, it is not always easy to neatly classify these emotions as good or bad. We must remember that it is how we use our emotions that renders them good or bad, positive or negative. On the one hand, the appropriate use of emotions produces feelings of wellbeing, happiness, joy, peace, strength, courage, love, and fulfillment of life. On the other hand, the inappropriate use of emotions brings sickness, weakness, discomfort, loneliness, frustration, unhappiness, sorrow, and emptiness.

Joy is associated with feelings of love, laughter, kindness, goodness, and acceptance. It brings forth enjoyable words and expressions, acceptable attitudes, and praiseworthy actions.

Emotions are based on feelings and are recognized by others through outward expressions. Emotions work together in clusters. For example, anger is associated with angry words, hateful attitudes, hurtful thoughts, frightening expressions, and rejection. It can prompt a person to proceed with actions based on those angry feelings without seeking the counsel of reason and morals. When strong emotions go unchecked, they can lead us to act without the guidance of the other two members of the second triangle.

MORALS

The morals member of the second triangle is an innate part of the human personality. It is associated with the judgment of right and wrong and is attributed to ethics. Morals are learned and affirmed as one's values. Reason is directly associated with knowledge, emotion is directly associated with feelings, and morals are directly associated with values. Morals are the basic governing agent of one's character. Therefore, moral development is essential for establishing basic values.

Morals are learned within families, religious centers, and schools. Family beliefs and practices have a strong influence on the early development of our moral values and character. Religious beliefs are often identified as moral teachings, and religious practices contribute to the value structure in one's character development.

There are accepted basic moral standards for social behavior regardless of religious differences or family practices. Social standards are necessary for all members of society. For example, truth telling is expected from all of us, in all situations. Truths are facts. One's moral ability enables them to judge facts as right or wrong for decision making. Right is acceptable behavior, and wrong is unacceptable behavior.

Acceptable and unacceptable behavior are associated with values, which are associated with beliefs. Beliefs are associated with one's religion and culture. Established beliefs influence the moral character, which in turn influences one's decisions. For example, it is right for a person to work and make a living. Therefore, it is right for a person to look for a job. In searching for a job, one crosses the national boundary and enters another country without permission. There she finds a job and makes a living. She knows that crossing the boundary without permission is wrong, but she may see others do the same thing, or she may feel compelled to find a job to provide for her and her family's needs. Therefore, her moral judgment is subjected to the influence of her needs and the social behavior of her peers. Another person who believes that crossing the boundary is wrong may be prevented by his moral values from crossing that line. Such a person suffers from poverty, and his children go hungry, but he abides by his moral standards. He struggles with the ethical issues of his decision: "Is crossing the boundary more wrong than depriving myself and my family of basic resources?"

A person guided by her acceptable moral standards quiets the struggle of her inner being caused by the members of the second triangle—reason and emotion—and goes hungry, depriving herself and her family of possible resources. Someone else may use reason and emotion to quiet morals. In this case, she believes she did not abide by her moral values and then suffers guilt. Yet another person may feel good, believing that he did the right thing to provide for himself and his family, and therefore suffers no guilt. The struggle within a person results from fragmentation between the members of the triangles. Decision making is an ongoing struggle within the inner being.

There are additional ethical questions: Who created the boundary between the countries and set laws about who can cross it? Why was the boundary left open for others to enter? Why should accessing opportunities beyond the boundary be forbidden? All of these and many other questions are processed within the mind to make the right decisions, which remove the conflict in the second triangle.

THIRD TRIANGLE: THOUGHT, DESIRE, AND WILL

The third triangle constitutes thought, desire, and will. These three siblings work alongside reason, emotion, and morals.

THOUGHT

Thought is the womb of the inner being, where ideas are conceived. It is the door for all incoming information. Thought is produced when the members of the triangles take action. Any member of the triangles can send information to thought. Thought can receive information through the senses of the body and from the stored information in the mind.

Thought sends the incoming information to other members of the triangle families for their counsel. Reason takes the lead in guiding thought into action. Together, they process the incoming information with the existing information in the mind and make decisions. All incoming information requires a decision, and thought is the mediator. "Thinking occurs between perceiving a problem and producing a response. For this reason, it is called mediating process."[8]

Thought processes all incoming information based on the existing knowledge in the mind. A child is born with certain senses. In the cognitive mind, the newborn child is aware of her mother and clings to her. It may be the mother's smell, the sound of her voice, or the way she holds her child that makes the child comfortable. Soon the child becomes comfortable with other caregivers.

The feeling of hunger is generated by the physical need, and the child cries for food. When the child grows up, she does not cry but asks her caregiver for food. As she accumulates information, she can process thoughts based on her needs, wants, and desires. As a youth, she goes to the source of food when she is hungry. Some families' food sources are the refrigerators in their kitchens. For other families, the source of food may be a convenience store or a fast-food counter. The child reaches for food based on her knowledge of where it can be found.

When the child becomes an adolescent, her sexual desires grow. Thoughts of sexual behavior must be tamed so that she may be deemed socially acceptable, so she learns how to control her thoughts. Morals, along with reason, help to process thoughts in an acceptable manner in the given culture. The morality of the adolescent's culture becomes the tutor for her behavior.

As she learns, her memory grows, and knowledge accumulates within her mind. This accumulated knowledge becomes the young woman's intelligence. Her problem-solving ability is based on her knowledge. She may process knowledge and program her mind as a critical thinker, ready to solve problems. She may become a creative thinker who uses her knowledge to create new possibilities. Such thoughts interact with accumulated knowledge and create solutions.

The Hebrew Bible and the New Testament point out that, by nature, we humans do not think in the way the Creator intended. We are prone to think in ways that meet our natural needs. When we think without giving room to the Creator within our inner beings, our triangles experience conflict. Such conflict causes pain and suffering, both to us and to our world. This selfish thinking is highlighted as the cause of the flood by which God sought to renew the world:

> "The Lord saw that the wickedness of humankind was great in the earth, and that every inclination of the thoughts of their hearts was only evil continually. And the Lord was sorry that he had made humankind on the earth, and it grieved him to his heart. So the Lord said, 'I will blot out from the earth the human beings I have created—people together with animals and creeping things and birds of the air, for I am sorry that I have made them.' But Noah found favor in the sight of the Lord" (Genesis 6:5–8).

Thought is the prompter for action. The above scripture says that "every inclination of the thoughts of their hearts was only evil continually."

A person's thoughts within the hidden chambers of their inner being is like the conception of an embryo that will be born as a good or bad action.

DESIRE

Desire is a natural process. The body seeks to meet its needs, and that action of seeking is the process of desire. Desire and thought are closely related and are often hard to separate. When the natural needs of the body are not met, desire prompts thought to act. Desire is expressed as a wish, want, craving, yearning, and hungering or thirsting for an object or abstract idea. It is strongly associated with emotion in the triangle family. Desire is the movement of energy within our living cells. This movement is the engine that generates energy for action.

A child's body seeks its wellbeing. Desire prompts thoughts of food, water, and other things necessary for the body's wellbeing. As the child grows up, new desires are born. The body generates natural-born desires—the needs of the body required by the growing cells—and the external world generates perceived desires. Acceptance and admiration from others are desires generated by social culture. As a child grows into adolescence and adulthood, desire seeks sexual fulfillment, companionship, employment, family, leisure, and pleasure.

Desire functions as a captain, directing our entire inner beings to accomplish our needs, wishes, wants, and goals. The intensity of desire drives our energy to accomplish its set agenda. When a student desires to be on the honor roll, he focuses on his studies to accomplish that goal. When an athlete desires to excel in his athletic abilities, he practices and learns the sport's techniques to accomplish his goal. Every person has desires that can be either good or bad, based on the person's values and the society in which he lives.

Religious and moral teachings are instructions to shun bad and wrong desires and instead follow good and right desires. In the Hebrew Bible, the desire for good things is good. God created a good and beautiful world. Therefore, a good life is filled with good things, for God is the giver of all good things and the fullness of life. We are to desire from God prosperity, a good spouse, a good home, good children, and all other good things. To please God, Hebrew believers practiced religious rules and regulations designed to align their desire with God's desire and will (the terms *God's desire* and *God's will* are used interchangeably in the Bible). During early Hebrew religious development, people made sacrifices to please God. Before God gave the Hebrew people His written laws on tablets of stone, they obeyed an unwritten moral code to follow God's desire for their lives. Upon receiving the written laws, Hebrew religious teachers gave further instructions, based on the laws, to follow God's will.

In the New Testament and in Christian theology, thoughts and desires are often used interchangeably. The natural mind is the prompter of evil desires. We are sinners by nature, and we have sinful desires. Jesus called for the conversion of the mind:

"What is born of the flesh is flesh, and what is born of the Spirit is spirit. Do not be astonished that I said to you, 'You must be born from above.' The wind blows where it chooses, and you hear the sound of it, but you do not know where it comes from or where it goes. So it is with everyone who is born of the Spirit" (John 3:6–8).

The Apostle Paul instructed us to use the mind for good desires:

"For those who live according to the flesh set their minds on the things of the flesh, but those who live according to the Spirit set their minds on the things of the Spirit. To set the mind on the flesh is death, but to set the mind on the Spirit is life and peace. For this reason the mind that is set on the flesh is hostile to God; it does not submit to God's law—indeed it cannot, and those who are in the flesh cannot please God" (Romans 8:5–8).

Hinduism, as well as Buddhism, teaches asceticism, or self-denial, to reduce desires. Those who seek Nirvana (eternal life) are instructed to go to the mountain and meditate to reduce the needs and wants that produce physical desires. Nirvana is the cessation of all desires. Christians seek the guidance of God's Spirit to fulfill their good desires.

WILL

Will is the commander of action in the inner being. It acts on behalf of each triangle family and our choices. "For when we say the will is the commanding and superior faculty of the soul; that is or is not free; that it determines the inferior faculties; that it follows the dictates of the understanding . . ."[9]

The Hebrew Bible and the New Testament both teach that God gave us free will, allowing us to make choices. We have the freedom to make good choices or bad ones, right choices, or wrong ones. Will is held accountable for our actions. It is not an independent commander, but one that acts on behalf of its army, the different angles of the triangles. The army makes the choice, and the commander executes it. The triangles make the decision, and the will is instructed to execute an action.

The principle of will can be illustrated as a battlefield. A commanding officer gives orders based on his knowledge of the battlefield. On the battlefield, soldiers face many difficulties. When soldiers get into a troubling situation, they contact their commanding officer, who then acts for the protection and victory of the soldiers. The commander acts quickly to save those soldiers in extreme danger.

A good commander is an experienced soldier who knows everything about the battlefield and seeks to understand the entire situation before acting. The commander does not act because of one soldier's demands, which can be based on fear; rather, the commander seeks to calm his soldiers' fears and help them become better soldiers on the battlefield. The commander is an informed servant of the soldiers. If he acts without the input of the soldiers, the commander will make mistakes, some of which may have terrible, deadly consequences.

In the same way, when we act quickly without regarding all the available information, we often regret the outcome. However, if we tame our wills to make the appropriate actions based on information—rather than the demands of emotion—we will not regret the outcome. Therefore, experience and discipline help the will to act on behalf of all the triangles.

Free will as volition is not the act of the human will but is God's gift to us that is included in the gift of life. As a member of the triangle family, will is based on the influence and decisions of the triangle members and acts on behalf of the other triangles. Therefore, to make the right decision, achieve inner harmony, live in the fullness of life, and to be in communion with God, a person should understand how the triangles of the inner being work.

FOURTH TRIANGLE: CONSCIOUS MIND, SUBCONSCIOUS MIND, AND UNCONSCIOUS MIND

The mind is the storehouse of information and is comprised of three angles, like three siblings. They are the conscious mind, subconscious mind, and unconscious mind.

The mind is an invisible, indwelling part of the body that does not occupy space, does not have weight, and has no substance—it is not made of matter. Matter, on the other hand, is a visible part of the human body and occupies space, has weight, and has substance.

"Some psychologists and philosophers who questioned the mind-as-substance idea offered the view that mind was the sum total of a person's conscious states. This meant that the mind was simply a mass of thoughts, memories, feelings and emotions."[10] Most scientists and psychologists associate the mind with the brain. The mind dwells in the brain, but the mind is an invisible force. Like a computer with great storage capacity, the mind stores information and can grow and expand without taking up additional space. It invites in new information and associates it with existing information. The mind acts based on the information it receives and already has.

Manfred Davidmann points out that the brain has two divisions that communicate with each other: "The brain is actually divided into its 'hemispheres' by a prominent groove. At the base of this groove lies the thick bundle of nerve fibers which enable these two halves of the brain to communicate with each other."[11]

The brain stores information in the mind as memories. Information is the key to communication. The communication process is complex. We communicate with both words and images from the mind. The left side of the brain uses words for communication, and the right side uses images. The brain retains information in the mind; some information is stronger than others. On the one hand, memories that do not make an impact on the brain are often discarded from the mind. On the other hand, some memories have a controlling effect on the brain. Both sides of the brain function together to achieve communication.

The brain is constantly receiving information and responding to it and storing it in its database, the mind. It stores information from early childhood to the present moment. Our knowledge is based on the stored information in our minds. The stored information, along with incoming information, is processed for communication, which is both verbal (words) and nonverbal (actions). The stored information manifests as both "action memory" and "abstract memory." Action memory helps a person remember how to ride a bicycle or drive a car. It requires the function of both sides of the brain. Action memories are deeply ingrained in the brain and require little effort to follow through with action. Oftentimes, painful abstract memories are discarded from action memory; they can grow old and disappear, unless they are refreshed. However, abstract memories stay in the subconscious mind and can rise to help the conscious mind.

Conscious Mind

The conscious mind, in computer terms, is the working file within the brain. First and foremost, the conscious mind seeks to protect, preserve, and provide for the wellbeing of the body. Like an armed warrior, the conscious mind acts against every threat to the body, responding quickly and automatically. For example, when a person touches a hot surface, he jerks his hand away within a fraction of a second to protect his fingers from burning. Sometimes, when facing an immediate danger to the body, a person freezes. The conscious mind seeks not only to protect the body but also to preserve it. It counsels the body to refrain from dangerous situations and warns it of possible dangers. The conscious mind seeks the body's wellbeing and keeps it in a comfort zone. It makes the body aware of hunger and thirst, so the body stays alive and growing. The connection between body and mind is inseparable. "The influence of the mind and the body on each other is difficult to explain. Some people explain it by discarding the mind. Others discard matter to explain it. A more common-sense view insists that they both exist and interact."[12]

The conscious mind not only protects the body from sudden dangers but also forecasts the possibilities of hunger and thirst should food and water not be available. It alerts the body of scarcity and abundance, of danger and security. To overcome fear possibilities, it offers hope possibilities, which show the many ways to secure safety, from scarcity to abundance. The mind is the motivator as well as the guide for the body's wellbeing.

In addition to serving the body's needs, the mind uses information to create new possibilities. The intricate use of information in the mind's reflective thinking can create products from existing material substances. The conscious mind uses the stored information and the new information in ways that it sees fit. For example, people long ago did not have mechanical devices. The creative mind used the available information and created tools, tools created products, and products changed the way people live and act.

The power of the mind is fascinating. As information increases, the mind can do additional tasks based on that new information. Cave dwellers had limited needs; therefore, their tools were limited. As they acquired knowledge, they produced new tools for new uses. We humans have created new products from the primitive Stone Age to the present day based on new knowledge and new uses. Information and invention run parallel throughout human civilization. Creative ability is a power of our minds.

While the mind is invisible and abstract, the brain acts as the physical keeper of the mind. The mind and the brain work together to enhance the other's abilities. Although the mind is not physical, research has proven that physical exercise improves mental ability: "When we exercise, particularly if the exercise requires complex motor movement, we're also exercising the area of the brain involved in the full suite of cognitive functions. We're causing the brain to fire signals along the same network of cells, which solidifies their connections."[13]

A healthy mind and body complement each other. When the conscious mind is unable to function, the body does not function well. Similarly, when the body is unable to function, the conscious mind does not function well.

SUBCONSCIOUS MIND

The subconscious mind, in computer terms, is the brain's backup file of information. The phrase *subconscious mind* is also used interchangeably with *unconscious mind*; this part of the brain stores information that the conscious mind does not use. It stays dormant without interacting with the conscious mind. At times, the subconscious mind acts as an independent agent without the knowledge of the conscious mind.

The subconscious mind holds extraordinary power over human behavior. It works as a rudder, creating fears and fantasies, dreams, and nightmares. When controlled by fear, the subconscious mind commands the conscious mind to act against the rational member of the second triangle: reason. Fear possibilities further create chronic anxieties, neuroses, and phobias, which limit our abilities to function in certain situations. When our subconscious mind interferes with the conscious mind, we cannot function effectively at the command of the conscious mind. Such conflicts make us indecisive and unable to act when necessary and may lead to mental illness.

UNCONSCIOUS MIND

In computer terms, the unconscious mind is the brain's deleted information file. However, no information is ever completely erased from the mind's database. Information in the unconscious and subconscious minds interacts without the permission of the conscious mind, producing various results within the mind. According to psychologists, imbedded painful information can rise and create images that interfere with the conscious mind. Neurologists, psychiatrists, and psychologists who study the unconscious mind have concluded that mental illness is caused by the work of the sub-conscious and unconscious minds.

"Freud observed that many patients behaved according to the drives and experiences of which they were not consciously aware. He thus concluded that the unconscious plays a major role in shaping behavior. He also concluded that the unconscious is full of memories of events from early childhood—sometimes as far back as infancy. Freud noted that if these memories were especially painful, people kept them out of conscious awareness. He used the term defense mechanisms for the methods by which individuals did this. Freud believed that patients used [vast amounts] of energy in forming defense mechanisms. Tying up energy in defense mechanisms could affect a person's ability to lead a productive life; causing an illness that Freud called neurosis."[14]

TRIANGLE MEMBERS HELP ONE ANOTHER TO BALANCE LIFE

We have only one body, one soul, and one spirit, but we have four triangles whose members function as many selves. When we submit our inner beings to God and seek His presence for balancing the triangles and their members, we experience the presence and power of God in our lives and relationships.

However, when tragedy strikes—the death of a loved one, financial crisis, any painful situation—the emotion member feels down, and the body tends to follow the emotions. In those times, the triangle members help to normalize one another. Reason offers realistic counsel to emotion, and morals joins reason with the affirmation of rational counsel. Reason may say to emotion, "Death is part of life; you cannot prevent it. You must make the best of your life. You must look after your children or others in your care." If the affected person is religious, morals invite God into the situation. The inner triangles counsel one another to make a person function normally. If a person cannot recover from emotion's pain with the help of the other members of the triangles within six weeks and experiences depression, it might be wise to seek professional counsel.

When one person is critical toward another, say, judging another person, friction within the members of the triangles ensues. To relieve the friction, morals remind reason that this critical action was rigid and unkind. If this person is a Christian, morals counsel reason to repent and be reconciled with the one he/she offended. Even though emotion joined with reason in the initial passing of judgment, in most cases, emotion accepts the counsel of morals for repentance.

When we are carried away by our religious involvement or church activities and neglect personal responsibilities, reason reminds morals to be realistic, that God is not pleased with busybodies who do His work at the expense of personal responsibilities. When we listen to morals' inner voice that seeks to restore balance, we often see that our actions are not guided by God's Spirit, but by our own mixed emotions. At this point, we can make needed adjustments, take personal responsibility, and correct our behavior.

When we experience fragmentation within our inner beings and ignore the counsel of the triangle members, we need God's Spirit to balance those triangles and their members. If we are not able to accept the triangle members' counsel and do not allow the Spirit of God to balance the inner conflict, we should seek professional help to heal our fragmented triangles.

STUDY QUESTIONS

1. Identify the members of the four triangles.

2. From your own experience, explain how the triangles are related to one another.

3. Which member of the second triangle is your first prompter?

4. Do you feel the presence of God in your inner being? Why or why not?

5. What is causing resistance in your inner being against complete obedience to God's Spirit?

CHAPTER

2

GOD AS A TRIANGLE

The Hebrew Bible, known as the Old Testament, begins with this statement: "In the beginning when God created the heavens and the earth . . ." (Genesis 1:1).

The Old Testament strictly teaches that there is only one God. Throughout the Old Testament teachings, this affirmation was instilled within the Hebrew people. God gave Moses the Ten Commandments, saying in Exodus 20:2-3, "I am the Lord your God, who brought you out of the land of Egypt, out of the house of slavery; you shall have no other gods before me," and in Deuteronomy 6:4, "Hear, O Israel: The Lord is our God, the Lord alone." The King James Version renders this verse as "Hear, O Israel: The Lord our God is one Lord."

The Hebrew people rejected the concept of multiple gods. However, it seems odd that the following verses portray the pluralistic nature of God:

> "Then God said, '*Let us make* humankind *in our image*, according to *our likeness*; and let them have dominion over the fish of the sea, and over the birds of the air, and over the cattle, and over all the wild animals of the earth, and over every creeping thing that creeps upon the earth.' So God created humankind in his image, in the image of God he created them; male and female he created them" (Genesis 1:26–27, emphasis mine).

"'Let us make man.' Here God is saying, '*let us*.' It is God in plural form. Many theologians and commentators think such use was showing the majesty of God. Other theologians think that the writer was taking the idea from Babylonian Creation Epic. Still other theologians think it was God taking counsel from the heavenly host."[15]

God did not need counsel from other beings. God is one and only one. God is a triangle made up of the Father, Son, and Holy Spirit. One part does not act without the counsel of the other two. The three are united, as the Nicene Creed affirms:

"We believe in one God, the Father Almighty, the maker of heaven and earth, of things visible and invisible. And in one Lord Jesus Christ, the Son of God, the begotten of God the Father, the Only-begotten, that is of the essence of the Father. God of God, Light of Light, true God of true God, begotten and not made; of the very same nature of the Father, by Whom all things came into being, in heaven and on earth, visible and invisible. Who for us humanity and for our salvation came down from heaven, was incarnate, was made human, was born perfectly of the Holy Virgin Mary by the Holy Spirit. By whom He took body, soul, and mind, and everything that is in man, truly and not in semblance. He suffered, was crucified, was buried, rose again on the third day, ascended into heaven with the same body, [and] sat at the right hand of the Father. He is to come with the same body and with the glory of the Father, to judge the living and the dead; of His kingdom there is no end. We believe in the Holy Spirit, in the uncreated and the perfect; Who spoke through the Law, prophets, and Gospels; Who came down upon the Jordan, preached through the apostles, and lived in the saints. We believe also in only One, Universal, Apostolic, and [Holy] Church; in one baptism in repentance, for the remission, and forgiveness of sins; and in the resurrection of the dead, in the everlasting judgement of souls and bodies, and the Kingdom of Heaven and in the everlasting life."[16]

The writer of the gospel of John understood Jesus's nature and purpose as he gave the account of Jesus's prayer in chapter 17: "I glorified you on earth by finishing the work that you gave me to do. So now, Father, glorify me in your own presence with *the glory that I had in your presence before the world existed* . . . And now I am no longer in the world, but they are in the world, and I am coming to you. Holy Father, protect them in your name that you have given me, so that they may be *one, as we are one*" (John 17:4-5, 11, emphasis mine).

The one and only God said: "*Let us make humankind in our image, according to our likeness*" (Genesis 1:26). The image of God is not flesh and blood but Spirit. God created human beings from the ground. He formed the body from the materials of the created world, yet the body did not have life until God breathed life into it. The breath of God is the Spirit of God, which has both a life-giving soul and an interactive spirit. Upon receiving the breath of God, man became a living being: "The Lord God formed man from the dust of the ground, and breathed into his nostrils the *breath of life*; and the man became a living being" (Genesis 2:7, emphasis mine).

The life-giving soul and spirit are contained in the breath of life. They activate the triangles and their members within our inner beings. The triangles and their members are the functional parts of our inner beings, so long as the soul and spirit are alive and active. The soul and spirit are intricately interwoven to interact with each other. Their actions cause reactions and conflicts within the triangle family and the inner being: the self. Soul and spirit are not capable of balancing the triangles' members to work together. Only the giver of the breath of life can balance the triangles and cause their members to work together as a single unit. When the triangles and their members are balanced, they not only experience life but also unity. When the spirit within them reaches out to God's Spirit, who gave life, the triangles and their members connect with God and experience His presence.

In summary, the Spirit of God, the source of all creation—comprised of Father, Son, and Holy Spirit, being one in unity—created all things visible and invisible within the universe. God gave us the ability to be creative and create new things. Our limit is the inability to create anything out of nothing. We must use existing resources in the universe to create anything new. This was God's purpose, to give us "dominion over the created world" (Genesis 1:28).

Unlike God, we cannot keep our inner beings—the triangles and their members—in harmony; thus, we experience fragmentation within. Jesus Christ came as the visible manifestation of God in the flesh to help us live harmoniously within and with God's Spirit while on earth and beyond.

God gave the Ten Commandments to the Israelites so they could live in harmony with one another and experience the presence of God. Along with the Commandments came this added responsibility: "Hear, O Israel: The Lord is our God, the Lord alone [one Lord]. *You shall love the Lord your God with all your heart, and with all your soul, and with all your might*" (Deuteronomy 6:4–5, emphasis mine).

Loving God is being connected with God, for God is love.

GOD IS LOVE

The English word *love* encompasses many different concepts. We say, "I love banana pudding," "I love to listen to her sing," "I love my garden," "I love my dog," "I love my children," "I love my spouse," and "I love God." The list goes on. These statements fall into four categories of love used by the Greeks: *Storge* means familial or affectionate love. *Eros* refers to passionate, sexual desires and longing. *Philia* is the word for friendship without sexual feelings. *Agape* is the love of God.

The Apostle John, the beloved disciple of Jesus, provides an exposition of the word *love* as the love representing God in the fourth chapter of 1 John:

> "Beloved, let us love one another, because love is from God; everyone who loves is born of God and knows God. *Whoever does not love does not know God, for God is love.* God's love was revealed among us in this way: God sent his only Son into the world so that we might live through him. In this is love, not that we loved God but that he loved us and sent his Son to be the atoning sacrifice for our sins. Beloved, since God loved us so much, we also ought to love one another. No one has ever seen God; if we love one another, God lives in us, and his love is perfected in us.
>
> By this we know that we abide in him and he in us, because he has given us of his Spirit. And we have seen and do testify that the Father has sent his Son as the Savior of the world. God abides in those who confess that Jesus is the Son of God, and they abide in God. So we have known and believe the love that God has for us.
>
> God is love, and those who abide in love abide in God, and God abides in them. Love has been perfected among us in this:

that we may have boldness on the day of judgment, because as he is, so are we in this world. There is no fear in love, but perfect love casts out fear; for fear has to do with punishment, and whoever fears has not reached perfection in love. We love because he first loved us. Those who say, 'I love God,' and hate their brothers or sisters, are liars; for those who do not love a brother or sister whom they have seen, cannot love God whom they have not seen. The commandment we have from him is this: those who love God must love their brothers and sisters also" (1 John 4:7–21, emphasis mine).

The word *love* is repeated twenty-seven times in this passage. There is a big difference between *agape* and the other forms of love. Agape represents God. All other words for love are associated with feelings, which are born of emotions.

Emotions are the connecting link in human relationships. Emotions seek fulfillment in accomplishing a goal, and they fluctuate depending on situations and circumstances. As we have seen, emotion is one of the members of the human triangles. Emotion needs to be balanced by reason and morals. We are incapable of balancing our inner beings without God's help. We are pulled apart by our rational minds and many emotions, including greed, prejudices, desires, and passions. These are the players in our inner beings who need a referee to keep the members from fighting one another and to help them work together in harmony.

Agape, God's love, is not an emotion. It is power. It is the creative power. It is the reality that hovered over the darkness at the beginning of creation. It is the force that created the universe. It is the power that brought order out of chaos. Agape is the invisible reality that can indwell within our inner beings. It is the purest form of love. It requires no payment, for it is unconditional and available to everyone. When we allow agape—the love of God—to control our inner beings, we will receive the power of God within us. With God's power of love within, we can balance life and help all our triangles work together in harmony. With such power of God within us, we experience a mighty force that gives strength, courage, and character. It enriches and removes estrangement in our relationships and empowers our marriages. It fills our inner beings with joy, peace, and satisfaction of life. The power of God's love within us provides for us the strength to love our enemies and gives us the power to overcome all destructive forces that try to conquer our lives. God's love, agape, must be the controlling force within our inner beings to bring balance to the triangles.

When we are fragmented within, we disconnect from the Spirit of God, the giver of life. This is what we read as the fall of Adam and Eve in the Garden of Eden. God was pushed aside when Adam and Eve decided to eat fruit from the forbidden tree. We all share Adam's fallen nature; therefore, we need to bring our fragmented inner beings (our spirits) and connect with God's Spirit. It is like an electric plug that must connect to the outlet—the source of electricity—to fulfill its purpose.

However, we are incapable of accomplishing this challenging task by ourselves. God sent Jesus to help us connect with God's Spirit. Jesus became an adapter for us, enabling us to plug into the great source of power. He came to save us and show us how to connect with the Father. Jesus offered the Holy Spirit to dwell within us and connect us to the Father. The Holy Spirit is the wire. Without the Father, there is no power. Without the Son, we are unable to connect, and without the Holy Spirit, there is no flow of power. The Father, Son, and Holy Spirit are one triangle, one united entity. The Father is the source of power, and that power is love, an invisible but mighty force. When we allow the Holy Spirit to dwell within our inner beings (soul and spirit), we are connected to the Spirit of God and experience harmony. This experience is what Jesus promised to His disciples in the Gospel of John:

> "'If you love me, you will keep my commandments. And I will ask the Father, and he will give you another Advocate, to be with you forever. This is the Spirit of truth, whom the world cannot receive, because it neither sees him nor knows him. You know him, because he abides with you, and he will be in you.
>
> I will not leave you orphaned; I am coming to you. In a little while the world will no longer see me, but you will see me; because I live, you also will live. On that day you will know that I am in my Father, and you in me, and I in you. They who have my commandments and keep them are those who love me; and those who love me will be loved by my Father, and I will love them and reveal myself to them.' Judas (not Iscariot) said to him, 'Lord, how is it that you will reveal yourself to us, and not to the world?' Jesus answered him, 'Those who love me will keep my word, and my Father will love them, and we will come to them and make our home with them. Whoever does not love me does not keep my words; and the word that you hear is not mine, but is from the Father who sent me'" (John 14:15–24).

On our own, we are unable to connect with God's Spirit and live harmoniously with Him. Jesus came to earth as a human being to show us how to connect with God's Spirit. He pointed out that we are controlled by the needs and demands of our bodies. We live for the wellbeing of our bodies, which is our primary object. We work to feed the body, meet the needs of the body, give comfort to the body, and create things to satisfy the many desires and demands of the body. In the process of living for the body, we create conflict within our inner beings and in our world. But, if we live with a purpose beyond our earthly bodies, we will enjoy the presence of God within us and live peacefully within ourselves and with the world.

The people of the Old Testament lived in a covenant established by God with Moses (Exodus 19–34). It was based on God's righteousness. The Hebrew people practiced the requirements of the covenant by offering prescribed sacrifices for their sins. However, those sacrifices became a ritual lacking the true repentance of their hearts. Jesus showed the people of the Old Testament a new covenant. He gave up His body as a sacrifice to help them understand the Spirit of God, the Spirit of love. Human beings can connect with the Spirit of God and experience the power of love for their lives on earth and eternal life beyond their earthly bodies. Jesus pointed out that the Spirit of God is eternal and immortal. When the followers of Jesus could not understand His teaching, they complained:

> "The Jews then disputed among themselves, saying, 'How can this man give us his flesh to eat?' So Jesus said to them, 'Very truly, I tell you, unless you eat the flesh of the Son of Man and drink his blood, you have no life in you. Those who eat my flesh and drink my blood have eternal life, and I will raise them up on the last day; for my flesh is true food and my blood is true drink. Those who eat my flesh and drink my blood abide in me, and I in them. Just as the living Father sent me, and I live because of the Father, so whoever eats me will live because of me. This is the bread that came down from heaven, not like that which your ancestors ate, and they died. But the one who eats this bread will live forever'" (John 6:52–58).

The Israelites offered the flesh and blood of animals as sacrifices to God. However, flesh-and-blood animal sacrifices could not atone for the sins of the worshippers unless they repented in their hearts. King David understood this and affirmed it in his prayer of repentance in Psalm 51. The flesh and blood of the sacrificed animals did not have saving power. It did not matter how many animals the Israelites offered. The spirit represented in the offering is what mattered most. Jesus says, "It is the spirit that gives life; the flesh is useless. The words that I have spoken to you are spirit and life" (John 6:63).

The self-giving love manifested in Jesus on the cross is the Spirit of God. Participating in the Christian sacrament of eating the bread and drinking from the cup is not for our physical nourishment; rather, it reminds us to make sacrifices of the body. Such sacrifice is a commitment to the Spirit of God manifested in Jesus Christ, a commitment to live in communion with the Spirit of God at all costs.

GOD BALANCES THE TRIANGLES

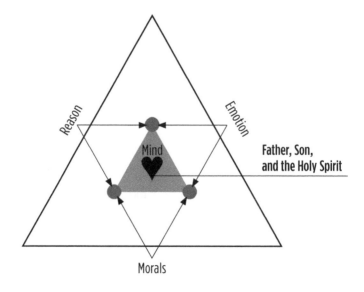

The Spirit of God is the creative energy that works within our inner beings and keeps the triangles in balance. The Spirit of God does not force its way into our inner beings. Our spirits invite and allow the Spirit of God to dwell within. If the mind submits to God's Spirit for guidance and counsel, the Spirit of God guides and controls the basic working triangles. When the mind does not submit to the Spirit of God for guidance and counsel, members of the triangles are free to interact without guidance or restraint.

When members of the triangles interact without the guidance of the Spirit of God, they join forces with select members of the basic triangle—reason, emotion, or morals—for action, alienating the third member of the basic triangle. Together, the two create a force that overtakes the third member and disregards its voice, creating conflicts within an individual's inner being. Such competitions are often subtle, like microscopic germs that cause fatal illnesses.

Only upon careful examination of the motives of each member can we detect the destructive force at work within our inner beings. Managing the conflict-causing forces of the triangle is the key to keeping ourselves from disharmony and fragmentation. These three siblings and their cousins need a higher power that will keep them in balance. Managing the inner conflict is a spiritual discipline. God must live within us and permeate us with the power of His love, agape. Agape must be in control.

TRIANGLES AND GOD

God, the Creator, gave us the freedom to choose between living in fellowship with Him or living outside of fellowship with Him. He endowed us with the gift of "free will." Living in fellowship with God is being in communion with the Spirit of God, participating in the creative energy of God, balancing the inner being, and experiencing inner harmony. It is allowing the members of the triangles to interact with one another under the guidance of God's Spirit.

Without the guidance of God's Spirit, each member of the triangles has the freedom to interact with the other members without restraint. They may choose and invite any member of the triangles to join their selfish purpose, or they may reject and alienate other members. The outcome of such action results in disharmony within the inner being, producing destructive energy—that which is bad, earthly, and unholy. This tension fragments our inner beings and affects our subsequent actions.

Creative energy builds up our lives and relationships. Destructive energy tears down our lives and relationships. Creative energy produces peace and harmony. Destructive energy produces fragmentation and disharmony. Creative energy empowers the members of the triangles and helps us actualize our potential. Destructive energy creates conflicts within the members of the triangles and limits our potential.

Spiritual discipline is the science of our inner beings reaching out to the Spirit of the Creator and keeping all angles of the triangles in harmony with one another. Spiritual discipline causes our intelligence to work with the creative energy, our spirits to experience harmony with the Spirit of the divine, and our beings to live in fellowship with God, fulfilling our potential. Spiritual discipline allows us to be online with God.

State of Harmony

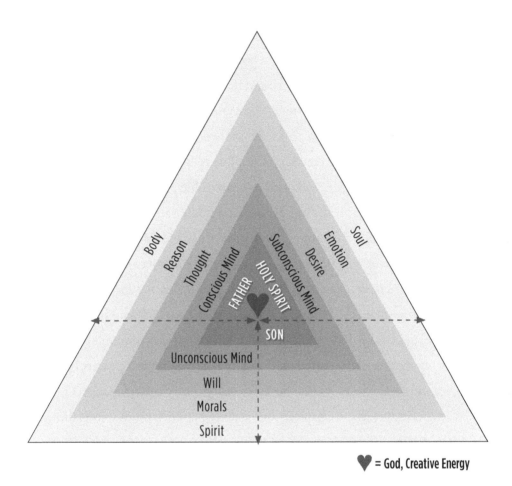

♥ = God, Creative Energy

This graphic illustrates how the twelve angles work within the four triangles of human beings:

- Body, Soul, and Spirit
- Reason, Emotion, and Morals
- Thought, Desire, and Will
- Conscious Mind, Subconscious Mind, and Unconscious Mind

The Spirit of God keeps all members of the triangles in their places of responsibility. Just like God is one (Father, Son, and Holy Spirit), we are one when all the members of the triangles work in harmony. The Spirit of God as the center of control within us can keep all the members in their places of responsibility without interference and fragmentation.

God is power, and we cannot experience this power with human senses. God manifested himself to us as the Father, Son, and Holy Spirit. His power was the source of creation. The Bible tells us in Genesis chapter 1: "In the beginning, God. . ." This abstract, invisible power hovered over the universe and brought order out of chaos, light out of darkness, and life out of nothing. God's power is unfathomable. It is vast and wide, beyond all human comprehension. However, it is also small enough to live in our most intricate parts, to keep us in harmony within and with one another.

God's Spirit is the controlling power that keeps all members of our triangles in place in this state of harmony. When our spirits submit to God's Spirit, all members of the triangles work in harmony. In this peaceful state, there is no competition within our inner beings, and we participate in God's creative energy. Here, we experience a state of perfect harmony and fellowship with God. The Bible illustrates this harmony as God walks through the garden in the evening breeze with Adam and Eve, the first human beings (Genesis 3:8).

In summary, no other source, thing, or power can keep the triangles and their members in harmony and help human beings enjoy the presence of God within. This proves the existence of God.

STUDY QUESTIONS

1. How would you use the triangle theory to explain the Trinity?

2. Can you identify your inner self as one but made of many members?

3. What is the difference between God's love and human love?

4. What is the correlation between the Christian sacrament of Communion and the love of God?

5. How can a person balance the triangles and enjoy peace and harmony?

CHAPTER

3

THE ACCOUNT OF ADAM AND EVE

According to the Bible, God is the Creator of everything. He created the universe and decorated it with the sun, moon, and stars. God brought forth life on the earth, both in the water and on the land, filling them up with vegetation and creatures of all kinds. After creating everything, God created the first human beings, Adam and Eve. God created them in His image to live in the natural world and have communion with Him. He provided the natural resources to sustain their natural bodies. He blessed them with the inner ability to fellowship with Him and live harmoniously with His Spirit. They did not have to choose the natural world against God's will. God's will for them was to live in the natural world, take care of it as stewards, and enjoy fellowship with Him. There was no estrangement or competition so long as Adam and Eve lived in harmony with God and the created world.

God placed Adam and Eve in a beautiful paradise known as the Garden of Eden and gave them power over all creatures, plants, and animals. The Bible tells us that God blessed them when He placed them in the garden, saying to them, "Be fruitful and multiply." The Bible does not say how long these first humans lived in harmony with God and the created world, nor does it indicate whether they had offspring at this time.

The writer of Genesis, Moses, did not focus on their harmony with God, but rather their estrangement from God and the ensuing fragmentation of their inner beings. Moses intended to provide a reason for Adam and Eve's estrangement from God and their subsequent sinful nature. This estrangement is often referred to as "the fallen state of man," which is the opposite of living in harmony with the Spirit of God. This fallen state is the broken relationship between humankind and God. It is the conflict within the members of the triangles. In the third chapter of Genesis, Moses focused on the event that caused the basic disharmony between God and the first human couple, and subsequently, all human beings.

THE FALL OF ADAM AND EVE

"Now the serpent was more crafty than any other wild animal that the LORD God had made. He said to the woman, 'Did God say, "You shall not eat from any tree in the garden"?' The woman said to the serpent, 'We may eat of the fruit of the trees in the garden; but God said, "You shall not eat of the fruit of the tree that is in the middle of the garden, nor shall you touch it, or you shall die."' But the serpent said to the woman, 'You will not die; for God knows that when you eat of it your eyes will be opened, and you will be like God, knowing good and evil.' So when the woman saw that the tree was good for food, and that it was a delight to the eyes, and that the tree was to be desired to make one wise, she took of its fruit and ate; and she also gave some to her husband, who was with her, and he ate. Then the eyes of both were opened, and they knew that they were naked; and they sewed fig leaves together and made loincloths for themselves.

They heard the sound of the Lord God walking in the garden at the time of the evening breeze, and the man and his wife hid themselves from the presence of the Lord God among the trees of the garden. But the Lord God called to the man, and said to him, 'Where are you?' He said, 'I heard the sound of you in the garden, and I was afraid, because I was naked; and I hid myself.' He said, 'Who told you that you were naked? Have you eaten from the tree of which I commanded you not to eat?' The man said, 'The woman whom you gave to be with me, she gave me fruit from the tree, and I ate.' Then the Lord God said to the woman, 'What is this that you have done?' The woman said, 'The serpent tricked me, and I ate.' The Lord God said to the serpent, 'Because you have done this, cursed are you among all animals and among all wild creatures; upon your belly you shall go, and dust you shall eat all the days of your life. I will put enmity between you and the woman, and between your offspring and hers; he will strike your head, and you will strike his heel.' To the woman he said, 'I will greatly increase your pangs in child-bearing; in pain you shall bring forth children, yet your desire shall be for your husband, and he shall rule over you.' And to the man he said, 'Because you have listened to the voice of your wife, and have eaten of the tree about which I commanded you, "You shall not eat of it," cursed is the ground because of you; in toil you shall eat of it all the days of your life; thorns and thistles it shall bring forth for you; and you shall eat the plants of the field. 'By the sweat of your face you shall eat bread until you return to the ground, for out of it you were taken; you are dust, and to dust you shall return.' The man named his wife Eve, because she was the mother of all living. And the Lord God made garments of skins for the man and for his wife, and clothed them.

Then the Lord God said, 'See, the man has become like one of us, knowing good and evil; and now, he might reach out his hand

and take also from the tree of life, and eat, and live forever'—therefore the Lord God sent him forth from the garden of Eden, to till the ground from which he was taken. He drove out the man; and at the east of the garden of Eden he placed the cherubim, and a sword flaming and turning to guard the way to the tree of life" (Genesis 3:1–23).

ANALYZING THE FALL OF ADAM AND EVE

The pivotal story of the Bible is the fall of the first human couple, Adam and Eve. Without this event, the entire Judeo-Christian Bible does not make sense. We should seek to understand this narration in its context.

According to this biblical account, God created only one human couple. They were naked but felt no shame. God came down to the garden and walked with them. This period marked the most harmonious state in Adam and Eve's relationship with God, the Creator.

A serpent convinced Eve to take fruit from the only forbidden thing in the garden: the Tree of the Knowledge of Good and Evil. The serpent assured her that the fruit was good for her, so Eve ate it and shared it with her husband.

Upon eating this fruit, Adam and Eve realized they were naked, and they hid from God. Like a loving father, He looked for them in the garden, calling out to them. God realized that Adam and Eve were now aware of their nakedness, and that they had disobeyed Him and ate from the tree that was forbidden to them.

When God questioned them, Adam, like a juvenile, blamed Eve, and Eve blamed the serpent. God did not ask the serpent why it had tempted

Adam and Eve. He cursed the serpent, then He cursed the woman, and finally He cursed the man. Once He had finished His curse, God drove them out of the garden and secured its gates with cherubim wielding flaming swords.

UNANSWERED QUESTIONS IN THE NARRATION

I grew up as an orthodox Christian. I believed the Bible literally and never dared to question a single word of it. Such unquestioning and reverent obedience kept me from exploring the greater truth beyond this simple story.

What we are told in this account is a serious matter. It is not just a matter of disobeying God and stealing some fruit. It is the story of our everyday, existential experience. God speaks to each generation through their cultural context and knowledge. There was a time this story was easily understood in the cultural context of an authoritarian father.

Today, we seek rational understanding. How could a loving God curse His precious children for disobeying Him just once and then forever kick them out of the only home they had ever known? That is unthinkable! What cruel father would do that? Regardless of how many excuses we make for God's actions, there is no justification for punishing one's children in that manner. Of course, generations ago, fathers could kill their children, thus justifying God's action. We should ask, "Is God such a short-tempered Being?" In the Bible, we are told that God forgave people of their worst offenses, such as murder and adultery. When His human family grew larger, did God become more tolerant? Does God change?

Let us look at more unanswered questions in this narrative. Why did God place a deadly tree full of attractive fruit in the center of the garden? Is

God the tempter and the originator of sin? If this is so, God is not only the originator of good but also the originator of evil.

When God created all creatures, he announced, "This is good." The writer of Genesis says, "Now the serpent was craftier than any of the wild animals the Lord God had made." What does "crafty" mean? Is craftiness the ability to persuade a person to do things they do not intend to do? Why would the serpent want to do that? How did the serpent learn to communicate with humans? If the serpent had evil intent, then had sin already entered God's creation? Moses does not answer these questions, and uncritical readers assume the serpent to be Satan. However, Satan is not mentioned in this account. The idea of Satan was not even available to Moses as he wrote Genesis.

How do we explain the behavior of a recently discovered tribe of people in the Amazon rainforest who live in nakedness? Since they do not express shame, are they free from sin? How long did Adam and Eve live in the Garden of Eden without disobeying God? Did they have children before they disobeyed God? If they did not have sexual feelings for each other, how could they fulfill God's blessed purpose for them to "be fruitful and multiply"? Did God intend for humans to live on the earth without conscious freedom, like incompetent people or puppets?

The serpent knew good and evil, but God did not want His children to know good and evil! It appears that God wanted to remain superior and feared that humankind, His children, would go to the second tree, the Tree of Life, eat of its fruit, and live forever! No, God did not want that to happen; He would rather see them die. Isn't it tragic? How can we characterize God as a loving Father when He does not want His earthly children to live forever? Therefore, children merely wait to die on earth to spend eternity with God their Father! How can they live in heaven with a God who forbids His precious children from reentering their home, paradise on earth?

QUESTIONS ANSWERED

The narration of Adam, Eve, and the Garden of Eden is unshakable and true. It was the human condition, and it is the human condition, and it will be the human condition, so long as there are humans. The story of human failure in the Garden of Eden is our story. This is our existential experience. Let us examine how this failure happened to Adam and Eve and how it happens to us.

Our every action touches our entire beings, either building up harmony with God or tearing it down. Sin causes internal fragmentation, and fragmentation produces guilt. Like immature siblings, members of the triangles compete for action. One of the members may join forces with another to overpower the third. Such behavior causes disharmony, distortion of the triangles, and pain in our inner beings. The Apostle Paul confessed his own experience of such inner struggle:

> "So I find it to be a law that when I want to do what is good, evil lies close at hand. For I delight in the law of God in my inmost self, but I see in my members another law at war with the law of my mind, making me captive to the law of sin that dwells in my members. Wretched man that I am! Who will rescue me from this body of death? Thanks be to God through Jesus Christ our Lord!" (Romans 7:21–25).

The event that caused the disharmony among the members of the basic triangle was not an innocent mistake, but rather a conscious decision of the first human couple. The voice of the serpent represented the created world, the natural world. The human body—constructed of the natural world—sought to sustain growth and enjoy the pleasures of the natural world. The natural body initiated the thought to pick up the fruit. It signaled to the basic working triangle to reach for the fruit of the tree. Reason found the fruit edible and emotion found it attractive. Morals remembered God's command not to pick the fruit or eat it because He had placed a boundary around this specific tree. God's warning against the Tree of the Knowledge of Good and Evil signifies the boundaries we should keep, maintaining harmony within and with others in the world. Everyone's garden has forbidden trees. To break the moral laws governing life and relationships is to pick the forbidden fruit. Reason and emotion joined forces and sent the information to the next triangle: thought, desire, and will. Thought sent the information about the tree to the conscious mind for possible action. Desire joined forces with reason and emotion, calling the will to act.

The conscious mind cautioned will, informing it that morals was not in agreement. Reason and emotion continued to work with the help of desire and sought compromise with morals. Reason, with the help of the conscious mind, advised morals to look at all the facts: the fruit was good, attractive, and edible, so why should a loving God forbid it? The conscious mind reminded morals of God's warning of the possibility of death—estrangement from God—upon eating the fruit.

At this point, thought became aggressive, prompting doubts about God's intentions. The voice of the serpent—"Did God really say . . .?"— caused the inner being to question God's integrity. Reason asked, "How can a loving God forbid his children from eating the good fruit of a tree?" Perhaps God wanted to keep Himself above His created children. Is that fair? What would happen if children became equal to their father?

Shouldn't a loving father wish for his children to grow up? The suggestion from the serpent was that, upon eating the fruit of the tree, Adam and Eve would become like God. In other words, when the mystery represented by the tree was removed, human children would be just like the Creator-Father.

Reason and emotion, along with the conscious mind, did not seek God for guidance and counsel. They continued to ignore morals, who prioritized God's command. Desire joined forces with reason and emotion and sought to quiet the voice of morals. These siblings counseled the conscious mind to act based on reason, ignoring morals. The conscious mind did not seek God's counsel to quiet the nagging demands of the other members of the triangles. Together, they persuaded actions without the approval of morals, ignoring the Spirit of God that kept them in harmony. Morals reminded the conscious mind, "You must not eat fruit from the tree that is in the middle of the garden; you must not touch it, or you will die."

Thought continued to engage in the possibilities of eating the fruit rather than giving up the idea. The serpent, representing the negative forces of the external world, prompted thought. The purpose of such thought was to divide the mind. The serpent introduced temptation, which could stay in the mind for a long time. Adam and Eve had to make choice: act with the guidance of God—represented by morals' voice—or act without it. Desire, along with reason and emotion, overruled morals and called the will to act and enjoy the pleasure of the unknown fruit. The body then enjoyed the taste and pleasure of the fruit while the mind experienced brokenness and estrangement from God.

Every member of the triangles is good and useful. When they work together, they become agents of God's creative power within our inner beings. When the members of the triangles reject God's counsel, they become agents of destruction. Temptation to act without the counsel of God plants a seed of sin—in essence, estrangement—within the inner being. Such seeds grow within the inner being and give birth to sin, bringing estrangement from God.

Hebrew-Christian theology defines sin as moral deficiency. The dictionary gives the following definitions of sin: "1) to break a religious law or moral principle; commit a sin, 2) to commit an offense or fault of any kind; do wrong."[17]

Sin prompted the conscious mind to doubt God's voice. This struggle may have occurred within Adam and Eve for a while; we do not know how long it lasted. Like an embryo, the seed of sin grew within and forged together with desire. As sin grew stronger within, morals became weaker. Desire helped the growth of sin and used will to execute the delivery. Weakened, morals could not prompt the other members of the triangles to first seek God's permission to pick up the fruit: "So when the woman saw that the tree was good for food, and that it was a delight to the eyes, and that the tree was to be desired to make one wise, she took of its fruit and ate; and she also gave some to her husband, who was with her, and he ate" (Genesis 3:6).

Reason might have informed the other members of the triangles that eliminating God's restriction and picking the fruit of the tree was liberating. Adam and Eve did not recognize that liberating themselves from God would have dangerous consequences. When they picked the fruit and ate, they broke the moral responsibility God had placed on them. Furthermore, Adam and Eve disobeyed and rebelled against God's instruction, thus rejecting the presence of God that kept their triangles in harmony. The result of their disobedience was the fragmentation of their inner beings. This is called sin, which is committing an act or acts against the will and guidance of God within our inner beings. To live in sin is to live without the presence and guidance of God. It is estrangement from God.

After eating the fruit from the forbidden tree, Adam and Eve hid from God. Estrangement happened within them before God came to meet them. Sin entered their inner beings and caused this estrangement.

The original concept of sin in the Hebrew Bible is described as "missing the mark." It is deviation from that which is good and wholesome. In this state, our inner beings are unable to focus on that which is good, right, and wholesome. Therefore, we are unable to shoot an arrow at the bull's eye.

When all sides of a triangle are equal, each angle is equally focused. When all the angles are equally focused, one can shoot an arrow from any angle and hit the target. When the sides of the triangle are unequal, the angles are not focused, and the arrow misses the target. It is sin that causes deviation and puts the target out of focus. When we sin, we do not allow the Spirit of God to control, guide, and keep all the angles in harmony with one another. Sin breaks the oneness with God represented by morals in the basic triangle. Therefore, because of Adam and Eve's sin, they find themselves outside of the wholesome garden God planted for them.

THE FALL OF ADAM AND EVE

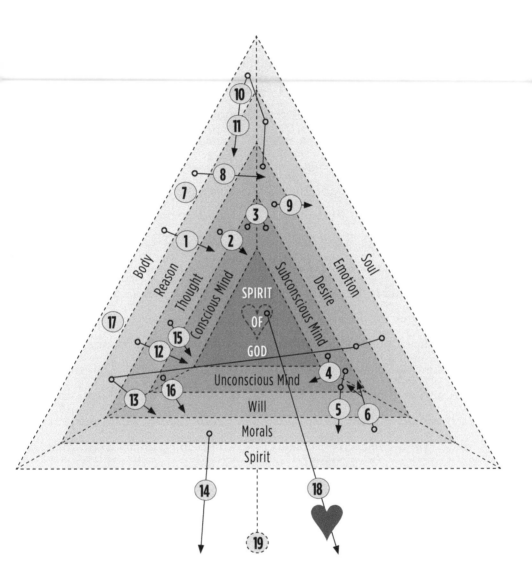

The body—made of natural substances—hungered for natural substances and found the fruit of the tree in the middle of the garden.

1. The body prompted thought to reach out and pick the fruit from the tree that was in the middle of the garden.

2. Thought sent this information to the conscious mind.

3. The conscious mind evaluated the information with the subconscious mind.

4. The subconscious mind sent the information to the unconscious mind.

5. Together, they approached morals.

6. Morals informed them that it was not God's will to pick the fruit from the tree in the middle of the garden.

7. The body did not give up and continued to look at the fruit from the tree in the middle of the garden.

8. The body reached out to desire for help.

9. Desire reached out to emotion. Together, they became a strong force.

10. The body's demand, desire's quench, and emotion's pull became increasingly stronger.

11. They demanded reason to reprocess the information.

12. Reason analyzed the information and questioned the integrity of the information within the mind.

13. Reason, emotion, and desire compelled will for action, ignoring morals' voice.

14. Morals was pushed out.

15. Thought informed the mind of the body's demand and reason's discovery of the possible discrepancy of morals' information.

16. Mind did not seek the counsel of the Spirit of God—which connected with morals—and gave will permission to act.

17. The body reached out, picked up the fruit, and ate it.

18. The Spirit of God, which kept the angles of the triangles in harmony, departed.

19. The members of the triangles experienced fragmentation, a broken relationship with one another.

CLOSER ANALYSIS OF THE FALL OF ADAM AND EVE

"Now the serpent was more crafty than any other wild animal that the Lord God had made. He said to the woman, *'Did God really say, "You shall not eat from any tree in the garden"?'*" (Genesis 3:1, emphasis mine). This thought first prompted doubt about God's command. The natural body originated thought. The body sent information to thought, who then sent that information to the conscious mind. The conscious mind then sent the information to the subconscious mind—the storehouse of information—to process the information into action.

How did such a question originate? Human beings, every one of us, have the freedom of choice. Eve had the freedom to decide—to think with the guidance of God's Spirit or to think without it. Thinking with the guidance of God's Spirit affirms God's counsel, keeping the angles in harmony and keeping in fellowship with God. Thinking without the guidance of God's Spirit allows the members of the triangles to act of their own volition. Acting without God's guidance breaks fellowship with God.

Eve answered the serpent's question as a matter of fact. Her conscious mind directed the question to her subconscious mind, who checked the information within the storehouse of her mind and responded. Her body did not like the response; it sent the information back to thought to reprocess and find a way to pick the fruit. This is the rationalization state of the mind. Temptation that divides our minds and offers an excuse to do the things our bodies like to do. It looks for loopholes. Every act of sin breaks the laws of God and makes us a victim of temptation.

Reason is one of the siblings of the basic working triangle. Reason directed the question to morals, who responded: "We may eat of the fruit of the trees in the garden, but God said, 'You shall not eat of the fruit of the tree that is in the middle of the garden, nor shall you touch it, or you shall die'" (Genesis 3:2-3). The question appeared to be simply fact-finding. If so, Eve had the freedom and opportunity to ask God directly. Her answer was not just fact-finding but doubting God's integrity. In her answer, she did not seek the answer from God in fellowship with the Spirit of God but sought to be independent of God.

Eve's answer marked the beginning of breaking away from the guiding Spirit of God. In this state, she not only rejected God's Spirit but also interacted with other siblings of the angles, creating conflicts within, and producing destructive energy. The members of the angles ignored morals' voice and together gave counsel: "You will not die; for God knows that when you eat of it your eyes will be opened, and you will be like God, knowing good and evil" (Genesis 3:4-5).

The narrative does not tell us how long the first human couple considered picking and eating the forbidden fruit. When the thought entered their minds, they should have submitted it to God's Spirit. However, they were not willing to submit the thought to learn God's answer. In this state, the angles of the triangles were free to manipulate and control one another.

When Eve saw that the fruit of the tree was good for food (reason), pleasing to the eye (emotion), and desirable for gaining wisdom (emotion, desire, and reason), she took some and ate it. The woman also gave some to her husband, who was with her (and in the same state of mind), and he ate it.

In their act, Adam and Eve did not allow the Spirit of God to harmonize the triangles of their inner beings. Reason and emotion—of the basic working triangle—worked together against morals and distorted the perfect angle, breaking harmony with God's Spirit. The result of this act was that the body satisfied its appetite and desire met its goal at the expense of

God's presence and fellowship. This is the fall. This is the human condition to which all human beings are subject.

The Spirit of God, at the center of the triangles, kept the members of the triangles together in harmony. Upon rejecting God's Spirit, the conscious mind became the agent of central control. Thought, desire, and will aligned and stood firm in rejecting the Spirit of God, alienating morals. At this state, the human triangles were no longer in harmony with the Spirit of God. The fruit of the tree satisfied physical appetite at the expense of inner harmony. Body and mind worked together and ignored the soul, ending in separation from God, which was a death sentence to the soul that outlasts the body and mind.

In every action, we are prompted to act by a member or members of the triangles, which can either work in harmony by the guidance of the Spirit of God or reject God's counsel. It is a human choice and a human decision. This is the existential experience of every one of us. We can allow God's Spirit to guide and maintain inner harmony, or we can allow the members of the body to take control. The Creator has given us "free will" to make our decisions.

Upon eating the fruit of the forbidden tree, Adam and Eve felt nakedness. This is the human condition. Until that point, they did not know shame. They were not afraid of God and had fellowship with Him. However, after eating the fruit, Adam and Eve became aware of their sexual feelings and felt shame when exposing their bodies. They were afraid of God and hid from Him. In this account from Genesis, Adam and Eve disobeyed, failed, and separated themselves from God.

The greater truth is that, upon disobeying the Spirit of God within our inner beings, we experience brokenness and estrangement from God.

AN EXAMPLE OF FALLING INTO TEMPTATION

Eric is the older son of his parents, Eric Sr. and Martha. He has three siblings and several nephews and nieces. The parents are older, but they do not want to live in a retirement home for the rest of their lives. They desire to stay in their home until their deaths. Eric lives closer to the parents than his other siblings. The four siblings get along well and frequently spend time with their parents. They are an ideal family, caring for one another and their parents.

The parents have sufficient financial resources, but they have not disclosed the details of how they want to divide their estate among the four children. None of their children are concerned, for they trust their loving parents to do the right thing.

The parents grow feeble and weak. They call their four children together and inform them of their intentions to have one of them take care of their financial affairs. They all agree that Eric, the older son, is the right person for the task. Eric agrees to take care of his parents' financial affairs. The siblings are also pleased with this decision.

Upon Eric's agreement, his parents call him and his wife Nancy to their side and disclose their financial information, instructing Eric not to make any changes. They want everything to go as they have planned and are giving everything to their children, grandchildren, and some designated charities. Eric and Nancy agree to follow their wishes.

Eric and Nancy are exceptionally good to Eric's parents. They visit often and look after them. Eric takes early retirement to care for his aging parents. His parents are blessed by his decision and they make allowance from their resources to compensate for Eric's lost monthly income. Eric and Nancy now spend more time with Eric's parents. Soon, they sell their home and move in with Eric's aging parents to take care of their every need. They are one happy family.

One day, Nancy asks Eric to think about their future. "When your parents die, what will happen to the estate?"

He gives her the details of his parents' wishes.

"Why such a large sum of money for charities?" Nancy asks.

"That's the wish of my parents," Eric says.

"Look, none of the charities are taking care of your parents: we are. When your parents die, the estate will be divided between the children and grandchildren," she says.

"We will have the house and the designated monthly income as long as we live," says Eric.

"Yes, but why should we give such a large portion of your parents' wealth to those charities? You should ask a good lawyer to see how we can make a change," Nancy says.

"No." Eric shakes his head. "I don't want to do anything that would upset Dad and Mom."

Nancy continues to remind Eric about his parents' estate, their portion, and his parents' large designation of funds to charity. After a while, Eric feels that Nancy has a point: they will not have as much wealth as his parents unless the large sum designated for charity changes. Eric does not want to go to a lawyer for counsel, but he allows Nancy to seek counsel.

Nancy visits a lawyer and informs Eric of the lawyer's counsel. "According to the lawyer, you must follow the wishes of your parents as prescribed in their wills. However, you can use all the funds you want right now because you have their power of attorney."

Eric and Nancy are tempted to take money out of the designated funds for charity. They do not share their feelings or thoughts with Eric's parents. They pray about it and feel that they should follow Eric's parents' wishes. However, as time passes, Eric and Nancy quiet their moral responsibility and rationalize that Eric's parents should not give such a large sum to charity, but rather, Eric should use those funds so that he and Nancy can buy a ranch like his parents had when they were young. They ponder this idea for months. Finally, they take money out of the funds designated for charity and buy a ranch.

Eric and Nancy always talk to Eric's parents about their decisions. However, they both do not say anything about buying the ranch. One day, a neighbor breaks the news to Eric's parents about Eric and Nancy's plans. When Eric's parents find out, they call Eric and Nancy. "Where did you get the funds to buy such an expensive estate?" they ask.

Neither Eric nor Nancy answer. This displeases Eric's parents, who ask him to give an account of his funds.

Eric and Nancy move out of Eric's parents' house because they no longer feel comfortable being around his parents. Eric's parents are heartbroken.

Eric's siblings learn that he and Nancy moved out of their parents' home and onto a new ranch they had purchased. Eric and Nancy do not talk to any of them. The family stops gathering at Eric's parents' house.

Eric's and Nancy's actions greatly distress Eric's siblings. The news spreads around town, making Eric and Nancy uncomfortable to gather with their friends like they once did. All those who knew Eric's parents are saddened by Eric's actions. Eric and Nancy's peers no longer accept them as friends and instead judge them as crooks who broke the hearts of Eric's aging parents.

COMMUNICATING TRUTH THROUGH STORIES

Truth is communicated in different ways. Sometimes telling a story to communicate truth is effective. The prophet Nathan used a story to tell King David of his sinful act in the book of second Samuel:

"And the Lord sent Nathan to David. He came to him, and said to him, 'There were two men in a certain city, the one rich and the other poor. The rich man had very many flocks and herds; but the poor man had nothing but one little ewe lamb, which he had bought. He brought it up, and it grew up with him and with his children; it used to eat of his meager fare, and drink from his cup, and lie in his bosom, and it was like a daughter to him. Now there came a traveler to the rich man, and he was loath to take one of his own flock or herd to prepare for the wayfarer who had come to him, but he took the poor man's lamb, and prepared that for the guest who had come to him.' Then David's anger was greatly kindled against the man. He said to Nathan, 'As the Lord lives, the man who has done this deserves to die; he shall restore the lamb fourfold, because he did this thing, and because he had no pity.'

Nathan said to David, 'You are the man! Thus says the Lord, the God of Israel: I anointed you king over Israel, and I rescued you from the hand of Saul; I gave you your master's house, and your master's wives into your bosom, and gave you the house of Israel and of Judah; and if that had been too little, I would have added as much more. Why have you despised the word of the Lord, to do what is evil in his sight? You have struck down Uriah the Hittite with the sword, and have taken his wife to be your wife, and have killed him with the sword of the Ammonites. Now therefore the sword shall never depart from your house, for you have despised me, and have taken the wife of Uriah the Hittite to be your wife. Thus says the Lord: I will raise up trouble against you from within your own house; and I will take your wives before your eyes, and give them to your neighbor, and he shall lie with your wives in the sight of this very sun. For you did it secretly;

but I will do this thing before all Israel, and before the sun.' David said to Nathan, 'I have sinned against the Lord.' Nathan said to David, 'Now the Lord has put away your sin; you shall not die. Nevertheless, because by this deed you have utterly scorned the Lord, the child that is born to you shall die.' Then Nathan went to his house" (2 Samuel 12:1–15).

THE STORY OF ADAM AND EVE APPEALED TO THE HEARERS

In the narrative of the fall of Adam and Eve, the serpent was the messenger of evil. The serpent has been the most deadly and feared creature in the Middle East since ancient times. Everyone realizes the deadly nature of poisonous snakes. How the serpent obtained its speaking ability is not the focus, but the moral, of the story: an attractive thought, with all its glamour and infatuation, may contain deadly venom.

We see, hear, and witness tragedies of sexual misconduct, marriages falling apart, and other illicit acts committed by respected and admired public officials, clergy, and others in our world. The seeds of their actions started with a thought, like Eve looking at the fruit of the tree in the garden. An attractive thought gradually leads to infatuation and turns into desire at the expense of marital commitment.

All thoughts should be filtered through the Spirit of God. Acting without the guidance and counsel of the Spirit of God is like eating deadly fruit, resulting not in physical death, but spiritual death. Spiritual death is separation from God. When we know that we are not following the will of God, we experience deadly separation. We are outside of God's beautiful garden, no longer able to walk with Him. Broken and ashamed, we are unable to enter the presence of God.

The man and the woman suffered not only from being driven from God's beautiful garden; they also experienced separation from God within their inner beings. Their fate is the spiritual experience of all who do not follow the will of God.

Jesus Christ, the incarnation of God, showed us how to overcome the temptation of attractive thoughts and live in fellowship with God. God indeed wanted His children to grow up just like Him, holy and wholesome. He did not want His children to make the created world their central focus, but rather the Creator of all creation.

STUDY QUESTIONS

1. Why did God create Adam and Eve?

2. What are some of the unanswered questions in the narration of the fall of Adam and Eve?

3. Explain why the author of Genesis used the serpent as the evil agent, Eve as the one who picked up the fruit, and Adam as a bystander.

4. Explain the fall of Adam and Eve based on the triangle theory.

5. Consider an experience of doing something you know you should not have done, yet you gave into the temptation and did. How do you prevent such a thing from happening again?

CHAPTER

4

Understanding the Bible

Using the triangle theory helps us to better understand the Bible. Let us examine two passages of Scripture, one from the New Testament and another from the Old Testament.

New Testament Passage

The Temptation of Jesus

"Then Jesus was led up by the Spirit into the wilderness to be tempted by the devil. He fasted forty days and forty nights, and afterwards he was famished. The tempter came and said to him, 'If you are the Son of God, command these stones to become loaves of bread.' But he answered, 'It is written, "One does not live by bread alone, but by every word that comes from the mouth of God."'

Then the devil took him to the holy city and placed him on the pinnacle of the temple, saying to him, 'If you are the Son of God, throw yourself down; for it is written, "He will command his angels concerning you," and "On their hands they will bear you up, so that you will not dash your foot against a stone."'

Jesus said to him, 'Again it is written, "Do not put the Lord your God to the test."'

> Again, the devil took him to a very high mountain and showed him all the kingdoms of the world and their splendor; and he said to him, 'All these I will give you, if you will fall down and worship me.' Jesus said to him, 'Away with you, Satan! for it is written, "Worship the Lord your God, and serve only him."'
>
> Then the devil left him, and suddenly angels came and waited on him" (Matthew 4:1–11).

In this account, Jesus was hungry, and He needed food for survival. Thought prompted Jesus to use His power to meet His physical need. Reason sent the information to the conscious mind, who made morals aware of both the need and the Scripture to support reason. Morals did not object but sent the information to the conscious mind. It appeared that none of the members of the triangle wanted to take the lead for action. Therefore, there was no demand to work against the love of God, which kept the triangles in harmony. At this point, will—prior to acting—sent the information once again to the conscious mind to examine and discern it, ensuring it was in harmony with God's Spirit. The mind, the storehouse of all information, checked the information with its other members, the subconscious and unconscious minds.

First, the conscious mind made Jesus aware that the thought of food was prompted by His physical need. Second, Jesus did not allow emotion to join with desire and create intensity for immediate action. He went directly to the innermost triangle, sought the will of the Heavenly Father, and found this verse: ". . . one does not live by bread alone, but by every word that comes from the mouth of the Lord" (Deuteronomy 8:3).

Third, Jesus used Scripture to guide His thought beyond the body's needs and demands to maintain harmony with the innermost triangle: the Father, Son, and Holy Spirit. Jesus, like the other angles of the triangles, could seek His will and break away from the Father's will. He could seek the help of the Holy Spirit, the other member of the innermost triangle, to persuade the Father to meet His body's need, keeping the unity of the Spirit. From the inner triangle, Jesus received the strength to keep all the other triangles and their members in harmony, beyond the body's demand.

Jesus could have used reason and affirmed that He had the power to turn the stones to bread and feed both Himself and the starving people around Him. If He used such power, then humanity would seek God for their bodies' needs at the expense of living in harmony with the Spirit of God.

However, Jesus submitted His mind to the Spirit of God to make the decision. He used reason and filtered His thought through the other triangles to decide what He would or would not do. Is bread for the body more important than harmony among all members of the triangles within the inner being? If Jesus allowed the need of the body to take charge of His decision, then the body would control His life. Such an act would not submit His angles—the inner being—to the Spirit of God. Since Jesus did not allow the body's need and demand to control His mind for action, He could evaluate, discern, and decide while being guided by the Spirit of God.

Perhaps He asked, "Would this thought and the subsequent action work with or against the Spirit of God, who holds the angles in harmony?" At this point, Jesus could evaluate and discern the will of God against His own will.

In Eve's temptation, she did not discern the will of God. Her desire for action intensified. She was not seeking fellowship and oneness with the Spirit of God; rather, she desired to be independent of God. Jesus, on the other hand, did not want to be independent of God. He wanted to live in harmony with the Spirit of God.

In both temptations, Jesus examined the information presented to Him without the bias of any member of the triangle family, discerned the will of God, and made decisions in harmony with the Spirit of God.

The Temptations of Adam and Eve vs. the Temptations of Jesus

ADAM AND EVE		JESUS	
Temptation	Answer	Temptation	Answer
1. Eat the fruit.	Good for food	1. Turn these stones to bread.	Man shall not live by bread alone.
2. Your eyes will open.	Pleasant to the eyes	2. He will give the angels charge over you.	Do not tempt the Lord your God.
3 You will be like God.	Desired to make one wise	3. You will have all these things.	You shall worship the Lord your God, and Him only shall you serve.
Result: Self-love controls the inner being. Experience separation from God.		**Result:** God's love controls the inner being. Experience oneness with God.	

The three temptations Jesus faced were subtle; they gave the appearance of working in harmony with all the angles of the basic working triangle. Initially, the temptations do not appear to be satanic. They do not even seem like temptations. Each question Satan asked presented an idea that would meet a need. How Jesus handled each temptation made the difference.

Adam and Eve failed in their temptations by not allowing the Spirit of God to guide them and keep the angles in harmony. Jesus, however, discerned the will of God in each temptation. In each test, He may have asked: "Who is the first prompter of this idea? What motivates me to act? Which forces are joining for action? Is there more information than what I have in this situation? What will be the result of my action?"

His first temptation was to meet His immediate physical need: hunger. There is no sin in meeting our physical needs. The difference lies in how we meet the need. The means by which we meet our needs can cause fragmentation of our inner beings. It was by discerning the results of such actions that Jesus became aware that the thought was not prompted by God's Spirit, but by His own body's need. Like the temptations of Adam and Eve in the garden, Jesus was also challenged to let the ends justify the means. As the beloved Son of God, Jesus could easily justify commanding stones to become bread to satisfy His hunger. He could have also exercised this power to meet the needs of starving people. Such action would have prompted society's acceptance of Him as the Messiah, fulfilling the prophecy about the Savior.

Jesus did not allow His own needs to divide His mind: He did not allow hunger pangs to make a decision to meet His body's immediate need. Jesus was committed to following God's will at any cost. His Spirit and God's Spirit were in harmony. Therefore, the Spirit of God and the Spirit of Jesus worked together to overcome the snare of temptation.

The second temptation challenged Jesus to prove to Himself and others the benefit of His special relationship with God. If He yielded on the second temptation, Jesus could have easily proven to friends and foes alike that He was indeed the Son of God and the Savior of the world.

In the third temptation, Satan asked Jesus to be God, to have dominion and power over the world independent from God. This temptation offered an easy road to the mission of the Messiah without being a servant. It was an attractive answer to the ultimate quest of the Israelites' deliverance from their oppressors.

In each temptation, Jesus sought the heart of God. Upon unselfish discernment, Jesus recognized that following through with such thoughts questioned God's integrity. Jesus did not seek His own dominion and power over the world apart from God. He did not allow any angles of the basic working triangle—reason, emotion, or morals—to take the lead and join with desire to act on their behalf. Jesus acted in harmony with the Spirit of God, which held His inner triangles in place. This was His choice. Jesus said, "I came to do the will of my Father."

In their disobedience to God, Adam and Eve ignored the Spirit of God that kept their triangles in harmony. They felt shame, experienced estrangement from God, and hid in fear from Him. However, through His obedience to God, Jesus experienced inner harmony and oneness with God.

OLD TESTAMENT EXAMPLE

THE ACCOUNT OF CAIN AND ABEL

Cain and Abel were the first two children born to Adam and Eve. They should have been the happiest people, living their lives while loving God, loving their parents, and loving each other. Unfortunately, that was not the case. Cain was a farmer and Abel was a shepherd. Both gave offerings to God. God accepted Abel's offering and blessed him but did not show favor to Cain's offering.

> "Now the man knew his wife Eve, and she conceived and bore Cain, saying, 'I have produced a man with the help of the Lord.' Next she

bore his brother Abel. Now Abel was a keeper of sheep, and Cain a tiller of the ground. *In the course of time Cain brought to the LORD an offering of the fruit of the ground, and Abel for his part brought* of the firstlings of his flock, *their fat portions. And the Lord had regard for Abel and his offering, but for Cain and his offering he had no regard.* So Cain was very angry, and his countenance fell. The Lord said to Cain, 'Why are you angry, and why has your countenance fallen? If you do well, will you not be accepted? And if you do not do well, sin is lurking at the door; its desire is for you, but you must master it.' Cain said to his brother Abel, 'Let us go out to the field.' And when they were in the field, Cain rose up against his brother Abel, and killed him. Then the Lord said to Cain, 'Where is your brother Abel?' He said, 'I do not know; am I my brother's keeper?' And the Lord said, 'What have you done? Listen; your brother's blood is crying out to me from the ground! And now you are cursed from the ground, which has opened its mouth to receive your brother's blood from your hand. When you till the ground, it will no longer yield to you its strength; you will be a fugitive and a wanderer on the earth'" (Genesis 4:1–12, emphasis mine).

Why did God accept Abel's offering with favor and not Cain's? The traditional interpretation is that Cain did not bring to God an animal, a blood sacrifice. The answer is in the narrative.

Abel took the best portions of the best of his animals and gave them as a sacrifice to God. By giving the best offering to God, Abel demonstrated his great love for God. In doing this, Abel showed that the absolute best of his heart belonged to God. He placed God first and at the center of his life. He was not controlled by self-love, but by God's love. Abel found great joy and fulfillment because his triangles were in harmony with God's Spirit;

therefore, he fellowshipped with God. He had an inseparable relationship with God and enjoyed the presence of God within his soul.

Cain did not show much love for God. He did not select the best for Him. His offering lacked enthusiasm. Cain merely met an obligation. He did not allow the Spirit of God to guide his mind and keep the triangles in harmony. Cain did not seek fellowship with God. Since he did not seek to live in fellowship with God, his angles were not controlled by God's Spirit. The members of his angles were free to interact with other members, and his emotion took the lead.

God's message was clear that Cain allowed his emotions to distort the basic working triangle and destroy the inner harmony; thus, God had no regard for Cain's offering. Cain became very angry, and his face was downcast. "The Lord said to Cain, 'Why are you angry, and why has your countenance fallen? If you do well, will you not be accepted? And if you do not do well, sin is lurking at the door; its desire is for you, but you must master it'" (Genesis 4:6-7).

The Spirit of God further reminded Cain that if he did what was right, he did not have to be upset. God warned Cain of the possible danger of allowing his emotion to take the lead. The distorted angles caused disharmony and fragmentation in his inner being.

Cain had no reason to be upset with his brother Abel. His brother did not do him any wrong. Cain's issue was within himself and his relationship with God. He was full of disappointment, jealousy, and anger. He allowed his emotions to lead his inner being rather than the Spirit of God. Cain could have sought God's help to subdue his anger and to balance his triangles. He could master it by allowing God's Spirit to guide his triangles . . . but he did not. Cain's emotion took control and distorted his triangles. He not only ignored the counsel of the Spirit of God but also the counsel of the morals angle of the basic working triangle. Cain's emotion and reason worked together, filling him with the destructive desire to kill his brother.

Did Satan make Cain commit murder? A careful analysis of Cain's mind shows that he was influenced by his own thought. He felt disappointment about God's rejection, which turned into jealousy—an intense emotion—against his brother, so Cain felt that he had to remove his brother to overcome his failure.

There is an ancient tale about a man and his wish to be rich. He prayed earnestly to God to bless him and make him rich. God appeared to him and promised to bless him. God said, "I will bless you as much as you wish, with only one condition: I will bless your brother twice, with the same blessing."

The man thought for a while and said to himself, "If I ask God for five hundred head of cattle, my brother will have a thousand head of cattle. If I ask God for a ten-bedroom house, my brother will have a twenty-bedroom house. If I ask God for ten servants, my brother will have twenty servants." He could not stand the idea of his brother having more than he did. He wished to see his brother poorer than himself. So he considered making his brother lower than himself. He asked God to blind his one eye so that his brother would be blind in both eyes.[18]

Cain's idea was to eliminate the competition. He pondered killing his brother, but after doing so, he could not escape God. The Spirit, who kept Cain's triangles in place, revived his morals and challenged his reason: "Where is your brother Abel?" At this point, Cain tried to have reason push against emotion and morals. Cain then lied and rejected responsibility. "I do not know; am I my brother's keeper?" (Genesis 4:9). He could not escape God, Who was the only one to keep Cain's angles in a harmonious relationship. Cain's fragmented triangles did not give him peace, and he could not keep them in balance. When there is fragmentation within the basic working triangle, there is restlessness in the soul.

Cain admitted his inner condition: "I will be a restless wanderer on the earth" (Genesis 4:14, NIV).

We experience disharmony when we do not allow the Spirit of God to keep our angles in harmony. When the members of the basic working triangle create desire and use other members of the triangles to overpower the Spirit of God, fragmentation takes place within the inner being, distributing pain throughout. Pain seeks various ways of escape in its search for tranquility. When no tranquility is found, the human soul hurts. It then reaches out for healing. A soul is healed only when the spirit of the individual is in harmony with the Spirit of God. The fullness of life can be achieved only by being in harmony with the Spirit of God.

Every sin is caused by a member of a triangle taking the lead, gaining support from the other members of the triangles, and acting on their strength rather than submitting to God's Spirit.

Every passage in the Bible can be analyzed using the triangle theory to better understand it and apply it for life and conduct.

STUDY QUESTIONS

1. What were the major differences between the temptations of Jesus and the temptation of Adam and Eve?

2. How did Jesus overcome His temptations?

3. Why did God not accept Cain's offering?

4. How does sin work in the human heart based on the triangle theory?

5. Select a story from the Bible and use the triangle theory to explain it.

CHAPTER

5

APPLICATIONS OF THE
BASIC WORKING TRIANGLE

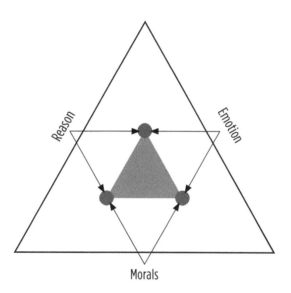

The Spirit of God is the creative energy that works with our inner beings and keeps the triangles in balance. The Spirit of God does not force its way into our minds but transcends within. If the mind submits to God's Spirit for guidance and counsel, then the Spirit guides and controls the basic working triangles. When the mind does not submit to the Spirit of God for guidance and counsel, members of the triangles are free to interact without guidance or restraint. Two of the members will collude to act, alienating the third member of the triangle and creating conflict within our inner beings. Such competitions are often subtle, yet they lead to sin and spiritual death. Only upon careful examination of each angle's motives can we detect the destructive force at work in our inner beings. Managing the conflict-causing forces of the triangle is the key to keeping ourselves from disharmony and fragmentation. These three siblings and their cousins need a higher force to keep them in balance. Managing the inner conflict is a spiritual discipline.

The members of the basic working triangle—reason, emotion, and morals—can become independent, egocentric, aggressive, and narcissistic, looking for self-interest even at the expense of other members of the triangle family. Such behavior causes personality disorders within the inner being.

"'Natural' narcissism, which is said to fight so valiantly against the inroads of a frustrating environment, is in fact verified by the sensual enrichment and the encouragement of skills provided by this same environment."[19]

Narcissism is self-love, and each one of the triangle members can manifest self-love and prominence over the other members. Such behavior is learned in childhood and at the stages of our personality development. The triangles are influenced by the environments and situations we face. Maintaining their healthy sibling relationship and ensuring they work together is the key to balancing life in every environment and situation.

REASON TAKES THE LEAD
AND ASSOCIATES WITH EMOTION

Reason + emotion = reason taking the lead and getting support from emotion while ignoring morals. What happens when reason acts as the first prompter and reaches out to emotion for action, ignoring the morals sibling? It generates a force that questions the integrity of established beliefs and values. This force finds ways to rationalize the objections of morals and overrules morals' voice as irrational. When morals' voice is loud and clear, emotion seeks to escape and to quiet the noise of inner conflict.

For example, it is rational for a business owner to want to make his business more profitable. It is rational to ask his employees to produce more and use cheaper materials to increase profit. Therefore, the employer's decision is based on profit. Those employees who object to this decision may be terminated from employment. The employer justifies his actions for the sake of profit. He does not exist to practice morality, but to make a profit. This man gives to charities and goes to church: not because he likes them, but to please his customers and to earn the support of his community. At best, he has little room for God, and at worst, he ignores God and gives no room for Him to balance his inner being.

In the same way, reason can dominate other members of the triangles. When the noise of the conflict within becomes annoying, reason seeks the help of emotion to ease morals' demand. Emotion helps relieve disturbing noises by offering pleasures. Reason, with the help of emotion, may find escape in alcohol, sex, drugs, sports, or anything else that overrides the inner conflict. In the case of the employer, the bottom line of increased profit quiets the inner cry of morals. Eventually, morals gives up its voice against reason.

However, when reason asks for the help of emotion and seeks the counsel of morals, it empowers all the siblings of the triangle to work together in harmony. This can be applied to our scenario of the employer wanting an increased profit. In this case, the employer listens to the employees and does not seek profit at their expense. The employees feel good about their employer and work together as a team, helping one another do their jobs. The employer-employee relationship is good and strong, like a caring community. The employer's profit increases, and he shares the profit with his employees. Such companies build up healthy workplaces and grow as profitable businesses.

As a husband and father, the employer keeps his personal behavior secret. He is loving towards his family and rational in his decision-making for them, but he ignores religious teachings. He may join his family for worship, but it is only to please them and win their approval. He does not give into the need to follow religious rules. He can be kind, even compassionate, towards others, but his moral behavior is not exemplary or praiseworthy: it is questionable.

REASON TAKES THE LEAD AND ASSOCIATES WITH MORALS

Reason + morals = reason taking the lead and getting the support of morals while ignoring emotion. When reason enlists the support of morals and ignores the voice of emotion, a person becomes rigid in his opinions and actions. He justifies his action by his moral values or his religious beliefs. This person has no empathy toward those who are hurting or suffering; instead, he finds reasons for their pain and makes subtle judgments.

As an employer, he expects his employees to adhere to a strict moral code within the workplace. He may not impose his religious beliefs on his employees, but he believes that good employees adhere to religious values. He does not tolerate anyone who breaks the rules, and he does not give second chances. Those who work under such employers feel like they walk on eggshells around the office. They show great outward respect toward their bosses but feel detached from them.

In this case, the employer's main objective is to make a profitable living in a religion-friendly environment. He may or may not be an active worshipper of any religion, but his conduct adheres to a strong moral code. He sees things in black and white, as cause and effect. He believes people get what they deserve, and he does not show his feelings.

As a husband and father, he is a provider who demands that his family follows religious rules. He explains why religious practices are important, but he does not express feelings of love or compassion. His spouse knows he loves and cares about her, but she is starved for emotional responses from him. When a family member hurts, he has a rational explanation for it. Even though he has strong religious beliefs, he may not express them in religious terms, but he sees everything through his rational beliefs. At best, he helps the hurting person to see things rationally; at worst, he is a judgmental person who gives reasons for others' failures and sufferings.

EMOTION TAKES THE LEAD AND ASSOCIATES WITH REASON

Emotion + reason = emotion taking the lead and getting reason's support while ignoring morals. When emotion takes the lead for action and enlists the help of reason, emotional satisfaction becomes the motive, and reason justifies the cost.

A person prompted by emotion seeks to assert himself before thinking. He makes statements and decisions based on feelings and often regrets the outcome. He seeks the approval of others and often tries to please others. For emotional satisfaction, he seeks escape. Those who follow emotion's prompts without the voice of morals can fall into the traps of addiction. They may become alcoholics, drug addicts, sex abusers, or sports fanatics. They may gain and lose their resources. They spend time and money on pleasure and excuse their actions with rational explanations.

The employer who allows emotion as his first prompt makes quick decisions based on feelings. He fails to give strict guidelines, and he seeks the approval of his employees. He becomes a likable boss, sometimes at the expense of his profit. At times, it is hard for him to fire nonproductive employees because he fears how others in the office will feel about him. At other times, he fires employees on the spot, without giving much thought to the outcome.

Often, he acts without having all the facts; then, upon learning them, he changes his mind. He is insecure and often feels threatened by religious and moral people. He avoids religious expressions at work and laughs at them. He makes statements like, "Church people are hypocrites." He will not submit himself to religious practices or self-discipline.

As an employee, this person does all he can to please his superiors, and he seeks the approval of his coworkers. He is a fun-loving person who believes that if people enjoy their work, they will be more productive. Therefore, he goes out of his way to make his fellow employees happy, even at his own expense. He spends his free time in fun-filled activities and hobbies, inviting his friends and coworkers to join him.

As a father and husband, he seeks a good time filled with emotionally satisfying activities. He buys things to make his spouse happy and is a lovable father who takes discipline lightly. His parenting is based on "what is good for the kids," but for him, "good" means "happiness." He goes out of his way to make everyone in the family happy. He spends money and time on his hobbies and entertainment but does not give to religious causes. He allows his spouse and children to choose the things they like and enjoy, so long as they do not promote something like religion, which challenges his perspective of pleasure. He sees religion as irrational.

EMOTION TAKES THE LEAD
AND ASSOCIATES WITH MORALS

Emotion + morals = emotion taking the lead, receiving support from morals while ignoring reason. When emotion takes the lead for action and enlists the help of morals, a person seeks emotional satisfaction with the help of moral values. Religion and beliefs become an essential part of this person's lifestyle.

This person is fluid in his approach, but argues his way based on his beliefs. He does not listen to the counsel of reason. He stands on his beliefs and becomes angry toward those who challenge them. He asserts himself with religious or moral values and often makes irrational decisions based on his beliefs. He makes statements and decisions based on feelings and often regrets the outcome. He mixes feelings with faith and exaggerates religious experience. He seeks the approval of others and often tries to please others with his religious experiences. He falls into the traps of faith healers, televangelists, and fundamental religious teachers. If he is not a Christian, he follows other religious teachings or substitutes religion for other beliefs. He becomes a religious addict, spending his resources on emotionally satisfying religious events. He seeks to convert others to his beliefs and feels good about it. He does not give room for others to discuss differing views. He becomes a religious fanatic.

As an employer, such a person makes quick decisions based on feelings. He wants to be a good boss to his employees and gives strict guidelines. He makes his employees feel that he is the boss, and his ways are better than theirs. He enjoys when his employees follow his beliefs and religious practices. He likes their praise and hates their criticism. He fires employees who fail his moral code. This person becomes a likable boss to those who identify with his beliefs. He fails to fire employees for their lack of productivity. He justifies his actions based on his religious feelings. He often acts based on his feelings without having all the facts. He is insecure within himself, and often feels threatened by the rational people in his workforce. He enjoys religious expressions within his workplace and gives his employees room for religious practices. He does not like those who do not practice religion. This person feels the need for preaching at his employees to try and turn them to religion. He makes statements like, "If you follow the path of the devil, you will end up in hell." He will not associate with nonreligious people or participate in secular activities for fun. He drinks only nonalcoholic beverages.

As an employee, this person is an easy-going worker who seeks to be likable. He freely expresses his religious views and beliefs with fellow employees. He goes overboard with his religious expressions and tries to influence fellow employees to follow his practices. He is not rigid in his ways, but he is not willing to partake in a rational discussion about his beliefs. He is threatened by his coworkers who do not practice religion. He detaches himself from those who are critical toward religious beliefs. His peers respect him, and he seeks to make the workplace a happy place with moral guidance.

As a father and husband, he seeks good times that are mostly filled with emotionally satisfying and morally acceptable activities. He buys things to make his spouse happy. He goes out of his way to make everyone in his family happy. This person spends money and time on religiously satisfying events. He is a loving father who disciplines based on religious teachings. He makes sure his children follow a religious path and religious teachings. He indoctrinates his family to think the way he thinks and to follow his path. He will not give them room for differing religious views and opinions. He does not spend much time on secular hobbies and entertainment, only on religious things. He can become a follower of televangelists, faith healers, and religious teachers. He financially supports these people and encourages his family and friends to do the same. He allows his spouse and children to choose things that they like, so long as they adhere to his religious beliefs. He sees the world through his religious beliefs.

Morals Takes the Lead
and Associates with Reason

Morals + reason = morals becoming the first prompter, taking the lead, and getting the support of reason while ignoring emotion. When morals takes the lead for action and enlists the help of reason, this person seeks to do the right thing at any cost.

His main objective is to be a moral person who follows certain values. Religious beliefs become an essential part of this person. He is rigid in his approach to life and seeks to be morally right and virtuous. This person seeks counsel from others if they share his beliefs, which are rationally based. He stands firm on those beliefs and will vehemently defend his position.

He is uncomfortable with others who have different religious views. He does not assert his religious beliefs and experiences on others. He does not make quick and irrational decisions, so he has few regrets. Before any decision, he seeks information and evaluates it before acting. He does not mix his feelings with faith or exaggerate his religious experiences. This person does not seek the approval of others and does not try to please others with his religious experiences. He does not follow every kind of religious teaching and often suspects the claims of faith healers, televangelists, and various religious teachers. He weighs everything before he makes up his mind. Even though he has strong beliefs, this person will not become a religious addict or spend his resources on emotionally satisfying religious events. He does not seek to convert others to his faith and he does not go out of his way to accommodate others. He allows others to discuss differing views and make their own decisions. He may or may not belong to a church or religious group, but he has strong moral values.

As an employer, he does not make quick decisions based on his feelings. He gives strict guidelines to his employees. He does not need to make them feel like he is the boss, for he is certain of his identity and is very self-secure. He does not seek their approval for his decisions and does not give concession unless he is convinced of differing views. He does not ask that his employees follow his beliefs, but he insists that they follow his guidelines. He does not look for praise from his employees, but he does accept suggestions to improve his business. His employees do not feel close to him, but they respect him. He gives considerable time for failing employees to improve before he fires them. He is prepared to explain his actions. This employer does not require religious practices at his workplace but allows them if they do not interfere with work. He maximizes his employees' abilities and gives them incentives for their performance. He may not go out of his way to help them, but he ensures they are treated right. He is very secure within himself and does not feel threatened by anyone in his workforce.

As an employee, he gets along with everyone without expressing his feelings. He does not spend time discussing religious matters in the workplace because he believes that it is not the place to discuss religion or politics. He minds his own business and follows the company rules. His goal is to be a productive employee. He has few close friends in his workplace. Coworkers respect him, but they do not feel comfortable engaging him in conversation. He is self-secure and has limited social interaction with fellow employees.

As a father and husband, he is a provider. He is not concerned with his family's feelings, but he cares about providing for their material needs.

He does not show empathy or emotional attachments to his spouse or children. For him, everything has a reason. He sees everything rationally: causes and effects, actions and reactions, choices and consequences. He does not lecture his family to follow his path and revere him. His emotionally prompted family members starve for his love and affection. They know that he loves and cares about them, but his lack of expression makes them feel detached from him. He stands as a disciplinarian and demands his family to do the right things and follow the right path. For him, the "right thing" is following a rationally based religion or his moral path while not giving into emotionally oriented religious expressions. He does not seek pleasure and does not spend resources on entertainment. He encourages his children to pursue creative hobbies and extracurricular activities. He promotes innovation, inventions, and new ideas. He encourages his family members to think independently and make their decisions based on moral values.

Morals Takes the Lead and Associates with Emotion

Morals + emotion = morals takes the lead for action and enlists the support of emotion and ignores reason. When a person's first prompt is morals while emotion is a strong supporter, the two ignore the voice of reason, and his moral values become strong and take the lead.

This person is a moralist and passionate about his beliefs. He freely expresses his faith and religious experiences, which he seeks to try and satisfy his emotions. He does not listen to the counsel of reason. He is mainly a nonconformist, and he searches for all kinds of religious teachings and worship. He wishes to live on "cloud nine" experiences. He asserts his religious values and often makes irrational decisions based on his beliefs.

He moralizes his feelings and seeks emotional gratification. He makes unnecessary sacrifices in the name of God and religion.

He makes decisions based on feelings and glosses over mistakes as though they are the will of God. He is often delusional and shuns rational discussion. He will not attempt to converse with non-believers who challenge his beliefs unless he knows he can convert them to his way of thinking. He mixes feelings with faith and exaggerates his religious experiences. He has the potential to become a preacher, evangelist, faith healer, or televangelist. This person seeks the approval of others and often tries to please others with his religious experiences. He becomes a religious addict and spends his resources on emotionally satisfying religious events. He seeks to convert others to his beliefs, which makes him feel good.

These people often run from one religious experience to another, searching for religious highs. They are "religioholics," addicted to religion. They are not interested in religious discussions that have critical tones or differing views.

As an employer, this person makes quick decisions based on feelings. He seeks to be a good boss to his employees and creates guidelines based on his moral values. He sees his mission as not only making a profit but also helping his workforce follow the moral path. He is not hesitant to preach at them. This person makes sure his employees know that he is the boss. He enjoys when his employees follow his religious practices. He likes their praise and hates their criticism. He fires employees who fail his moral code. He is a likable boss to those who identify with his beliefs, and he fails to fire these employees for lack of productivity. Often, this person acts on his feelings without having all the facts. He is insecure within himself and often feels threatened by the rational people in his workforce. He enjoys religious expressions in his workplace and listens to stories of religious experiences. He does not like those who do not practice religion. He will not promote nonreligious events or activities at his workplace. He enjoys fun if it falls within his moral guidelines and promotes religious expression.

As an employee, he likes to get along with his coworkers. He lives by religious expressions, and some fellow employees feel uncomfortable with him. He does not go to social events or parties for fun, where religion is ridiculed, but invites fellow employees to emotionally satisfying religious events. He feels threatened by fellow employees who are critical toward religious expressions.

As a father and husband, he is the religious leader of his family. He seeks good times—which are mostly full of moral teachings and religious expressions—for himself and his family. He spends money and time on religious things. He buys things to make his spouse happy. He goes out of his way to make everyone in the family happy so long as they follow his path. He discourages his children from attending nonreligious events for fun. He seeks to protect them from the "bad influences" of society. He makes sure his children are reared with religious values. He will not promote independent thinking. He is a loving father, and his discipline is based on religious teachings. He preaches at his family to keep them on the right path—according to his beliefs—and he makes sure his children follow his religious teachings. He will not give them room for differing religious views and opinions, but he praises them when their religious experiences identify with his own.

He is a self-righteous person and pronounces moral judgments like, "You shall not do that; if you do that, you will go to hell," and "You are not living by the book; that is the reason for your pain and suffering." He uses religious beliefs as a quick fix to solve problems, but this stems from false confidence based on his emotional attachment to religion.

AN EXAMPLE OF ACTION
PROMPTED BY THE FIRST PROMPTER

Brad met Kimberly in the hospital while he recovered from an accident. Kimberly was his nurse, and they were both attracted to each other. Kimberly took care of Brad's medical needs, and Brad was incredibly grateful to her. Every day, Kimberly looked forward to going to work, and Brad looked forward to seeing her. They exchanged phone numbers, and Kimberly often called Brad to check on him when she was not on duty.

They both were glad when Brad was discharged from the hospital. Kimberly went over to his apartment and kept it clean. Their friendship grew into romance, and they started dating and spending more time with each other. After six months, Kimberly expressed her desire to marry Brad, but Brad wanted to put it off to save money for their wedding expenses. Kimberly said that she could get financial help from her parents, but Brad did not like that idea. He wanted the two of them to save money and pay for the wedding themselves.

As an engineer, he was frugal with his finances and did not like Kimberly's spontaneously spending money.

Brad did not buy flowers to surprise her when he came back after a business trip. Kimberly knew that he was saving money for the wedding and did not say anything to make him feel bad. When he did not call her, she called him and chided him for not calling her. She liked to have some romantic getaways, but he felt they were unnecessary. Still, he occasionally gave in to her cravings.

Two years later, they were married, and they covered all the expenses themselves. Brad pointed out that, if they saved for a down payment, they could move out of the apartment and buy a house. A year later, they bought their first home.

Kimberly wanted to have a child, but Brad was not ready. He wanted to put off having a child for a couple more years.

Kimberly was often verbal and expressive, but Brad was quiet and matter-of-fact. They went to church, often at Kimberly's prompting. She liked the contemporary worship of a nondenominational church, but Brad liked the formal worship and the liturgies of the Episcopal faith. They compromised and joined a Methodist church.

One Sunday, they went to church and invited a couple of friends to their home that afternoon to watch a ball game. While they watched the game, Kimberly left the room to answer a call. She returned, sobbing.

"Honey, what's the matter?" Brad asked.

"Mom called and said that Grandma was ill and was taken to the hospital."

"Is it an emergency?" Brad said.

"No, Mom said she will call back when she knows more."

"I'm glad they've taken her to the hospital where she will get the help she needs," Brad said, then continued watching the game.

One of the friends who was watching the game with Brad got up and hugged Kimberly.

Kimberly felt lonely when Brad did not hug her or comfort her in any way.

Kimberly and Brad grew apart emotionally. Kimberly often cried. They went to a marriage counselor who helped them to discover their personality traits and their first prompts of responses.

As you may have guessed, Brad is more rational, and his first prompt is reason. In the case of Kimberly's grandmother, his response is that, if the grandmother is sick, let the doctors and the hospital take care of her. However, Kimberly is emotional, and therefore needs an emotional response. She needs Brad to get up, hug her, and say, "Honey, I am so sorry."

Only then could he make a rational response, such as, "I am sure the doctors and the hospital will take good care of her."

A person's response is often based on the first prompt of the basic working triangle. The triangle members are the basic contributors of our personality traits. The triangle members keep us in our comfort zones. However, building healthy relationships requires us to move out of our comfort zones to accommodate the needs of others. You must know your first prompt to understand who you are and how you should respond in different situations.

SUMMARY OF THE BASIC WORKING TRIANGLE

Each person is a unique creation, a natural being with gifts and abilities that can fulfill their potential. God has given each of us the freedom to use our gifts and abilities as we please. The basic working triangle and the associated triangle members work within each of us to set our paths as we see fit. Allowing God to balance our personality traits in our inner beings is the key to living in harmony within, with God, with others, and with the created world.

In the temptations of Adam and Eve and Jesus Christ, the first tempting thoughts were prompted by food. The physical body needs food because it is made of natural substances and influenced by natural elements. Therefore, the body seeks to sustain and thrive on natural resources. We cannot exist without food. Therefore, food and other natural substances become more important and more urgent to us than the needs of the spiritual inner being. Physical survival becomes more important than spiritual survival.

The body also needs to reproduce. When human beings live with only the basic needs of personal survival and reproduction, we become like any other creature in the world. However, the reflective thought power and transcendental ability of our spirits make us different from all the other creatures. The need to live in harmony with the Spirit of God is not a survival need, and thus it often becomes a secondary need. Therefore, we often give priority to food, sex, and physical comfort over spiritual harmony.

In the account of the fall of Adam and Eve, it was the body that prompted the thought of eating the fruit of the forbidden tree. Thought did not seek counsel from the Spirit of God; instead, it consulted reason. Reason did not seek counsel from the Spirit of God; rather, it consulted morals for an answer. The body was not satisfied by the response of morals, so it prompted reason to seek additional help. At this point, reason took the lead and reached out to emotion for help. Working together, reason and emotion questioned the integrity of God, the Creator, and reached out to desire for help. Desire joined the team and added enough power for action. Together, these five angles approached the mind, and the mind did not seek counsel from the innermost triangle—the Spirit of God—that kept all the triangles in harmony. Mind evaluated the situation with the help of reason, which said, "The fruit is good for food," while emotion said, "It is attractive." The teamwork of the body, thought, reason, emotion, and desire created intensity in the mind, prompting action. They all ignored the counsel of morals. Reason then joined with desire a second time and made an attractive appeal to the mind to acquire knowledge independent of God. At this point, the mind did not seek the counsel of the Spirit of God, but instead prompted the will to act. By this action, the mind and all the prompting members of the inner being separated from God, and, without a central control, became participants of misguided interactions and destructive decisions.

Every human action can be analyzed using the triangles to see whether that action is building up harmony with God's Spirit or breaking it down, whether it is constructive or destructive, good or evil, godly or satanic.

STUDY QUESTIONS

1. Can you recognize the controlling nature of the triangle members?

2. How do the controlling members of the triangle work in human personality?

3. Identify and state the leading member of the triangle within you.

4. Based on the working of triangle members, identify how you behave.

5. Based on the example of Brad and Kimberly, what changes do you need to make in your relationships?

CHAPTER

6

DISCIPLINE TO ACTUALIZE
THE FULLNESS OF LIFE

Three tiers influence a person: the external, the internal, and the spiritual. The external influence comes from the external world, the internal influence comes from within the individual, and the spiritual influence is of the Creator. These influences can be summarized in the following statements:

1. Life is a precious gift from the Creator.

2. The Creator has invested resources in each person and gives them the freedom of choice.

3. Each person must understand the purpose of life and have a purpose for their life.

4. Fulfilling the purpose of life with the purpose of the Creator provides fulfillment.

5. Internal inhibitions are innate, and learned negative factors influence the members of the triangles, creating conflicts within the inner being and limiting a person's potential. Internal inhibitions are fears, restrictions, taboos, beliefs, and other contributing negative factors.

6. External frictions are disharmony born out of relationships with others, the immediate world, the universe, and all that are in it.

7. Removing the internal inhibitions and external frictions is important for the actualization of one's purpose.

8. Each person must draw power from the innermost triangle—the creative energy—and subdue their internal inhibitions and external frictions to fulfill the purpose of life.

9. Spiritual discipline keeps the invisible line of connection between the human spirit and the creative energy.

10. Spiritual discipline is the science of keeping the inner being in harmony with the Spirit of the Creator to fulfill the purpose of life with the purpose of the Creator. It is transcending the human spirit to the divine Spirit and drawing on creative energy. Spiritual discipline is integrating the basic working files of the human triangles with the master file of the Creator.

PROCESS OF ACTION

Since the human body needs natural substances for survival, it is connected to nature. Therefore, the body seeks security in possessing the natural substance.

We use the five senses of the body—sight, sound, touch, smell, and taste—to receive information from the natural world. Within the body are the triangles of interactive members made of unnatural substances. These internal members seek to regulate the body's needs, demands, and desires.

The senses receive information from the external world and pass them to the members of the triangles in the internal world. The gatekeeper of the internal world is the triangle made of reason, emotion, and morals.

The triangle of the human mind is like a supercomputer. Active, accumulated files of information reside in the storehouse of the conscious mind.

Inactive files of information lie in the subconscious mind, and dormant, inactive files of information sit in the recycling bin of the unconscious mind. The active files of information interact with incoming new information and pass it on to other members of the triangles for appropriate responses. The files of information in the mind continually grow as the active files interact with new information and give responses. The result of such interactions is knowledge, which remains as stored information in the mind. Wisdom is the right application of knowledge; it is based on the information in the mind and is guided by the Spirit of the Creator of the natural world. Spiritual discipline is to live in and interact with the natural world in harmony with the Creator of said natural world.

The human body—made of flesh and blood—needs natural substances for survival, security, reproduction, leisure, and pleasure. It reaches out to the natural world to meet these needs, and in that process the body interacts with other forms of life in the natural world. For its survival, the body must consume natural substances—food—which takes away other lives: those of plants and animals. Whenever a life is taken, it causes pain.

Christianity, which is derived from Judaism, teaches that God created human beings to be the caretakers of the natural world. We are responsible for living in harmony with God's Spirit, fulfilling our potential, and making the created world a better place for all living things. When life departs from the natural body, we then enter eternal life. Christianity also teaches that eternal life is the gift of the Creator and that we do not obtain eternal life, or "salvation," by our own work but only by God's grace, which is the overflowing love of God. This love forgives sins (mistakes and failures) and connects our spirits with God's Spirit. A Christian life manifests the love of God and becomes a conduit of God's love in the world. We are to seek actively and earnestly to connect other lives with the love of God when we follow Christ.

Christian teaching calls attention to the visible manifestations of God's love through Jesus of Nazareth. Jesus acts as God's open invitation to all people to connect with God's Spirit and manifest God's love; Christians are called to do what Jesus did when He was on earth. Being connected with God's Spirit is salvation, and that salvation is available to all people. Salvation is the redemption from the negative influences of the material world; it enables us to participate with the Spirit of the Creator. Jesus Christ stands as the mediator between God and humans. His mediation is like an electric wire plugging into the source of electric power. Only through the Spirit of Jesus can we enter the Spirit of the Creator and receive eternal life, where we become one with the Spirit of God forever. The love manifested through Jesus of Nazareth is God's overflowing love, known as grace. Regardless of one's work, actions, or deeds, God's grace is available to all people, through Jesus. Though this principle may make it seem like we can live any way we want and still attain salvation, the Apostle Paul challenges Christians to understand grace as God's gift for living a responsible, God-centered life that draws energy from the inner triangle made of Father, Son, and the Holy Spirit:

> "What then? Should we sin because we are not under law but under grace? By no means! Do you not know that if you present yourselves to anyone as obedient slaves, you are slaves of the one whom you obey, either of sin, which leads to death, or of obedience, which leads to righteousness? But thanks be to God that you, having once been slaves of sin, have become obedient from the heart to the form of teaching to which you were entrusted, and that you, having been set free from sin, have become slaves of righteousness. I am speaking in human terms because of your natural limitations. For just as you once presented your members

as slaves to impurity and to greater and greater iniquity, so now present your members as slaves to righteousness for sanctification" (Romans 6:15–19).

The Christian faith calls for spiritual discipline. Christianity without spiritual discipline does not allow the Spirit of God to lead and guide one's life. A life without spiritual discipline does not live in harmony with the Spirit of the Creator.

JESUS IS THE MASTER TEACHER

Jesus Christ is the Master Teacher. He challenged His followers to climb the mountain of perfection: "Be perfect, therefore, as your heavenly Father is perfect" (Matthew 5:48).

Did Jesus challenge His disciples to aim for the impossible? No. Jesus practiced the way of perfection and showed us how to follow. It is not an easy road to travel. He said, "Enter through the narrow gate; for the gate is wide and the road is easy that leads to destruction, and there are many who take it. For the gate is narrow and the road is hard that leads to life, and there are few who find it" (Matthew 7:13–14).

Submitting our inner triangles, and all their members, to the Spirit of God is not easy. The members of the triangle family resist submitting to God. They seek independence from God. Those people who take the high road to spiritual discipline will discover the creative power of God leading them to fulfill their purpose for life with the purpose of God.

The first step of spiritual discipline is to activate the Spirit of God within the inner being. The Spirit of God is more than religious knowledge. It is the creative energy: God's Spirit. The Spirit of God is love. Our minds must commit to the fact that the Spirit of God will guide every action of our inner beings. Like checking a document for spelling errors, the Spirit of God—if we allow Him—filters every thought that leads to action. Members of the triangles, working together in harmony with the Spirit of God, help make the right response. Will must promise to the members of the triangles that it will not prompt action without first submitting information to the master file of God's Spirit, the creative energy of divine love. This is living in submission to God's Spirit. It is the experience of being born again, a radical transformation.

Jesus showed how us to live in submission through His baptism. Even though Jesus was a good man and followed the religious teachings from His childhood, He had to make a personal commitment and enter a new relationship with God. His baptism was His submission and His statement that He would allow the Spirit of God to overwrite His desires. God's Spirit, the love file, would be Jesus's master file, and all other files of His inner being would be controlled by God's Spirit. Upon His submission He heard "a voice from heaven [say]: 'This is my Son, the Beloved, with whom I am well pleased'" (Matthew 3:17).

Submission is the mark of a transformed life. The newly activated file—the Spirit of God—is Lord and Master over all the other files within our inner beings. Living a life of spiritual discipline is to live in the love of God and participate in the creative energy of God.

The second step of spiritual discipline is to learn how to employ the new file over the old files and integrate the new file to process all the incoming information—old and new—in harmony with God's Spirit for action. This spiritual discipline enables us to enter a personal commitment with a clear understanding of our purpose for life. A purpose statement is the mission statement of life. Jesus had a purpose statement for life. At the age of twelve, He stated it to His parents.

When Jesus was twelve years old, He went with His parents to the temple in Jerusalem for the festival of Passover. After the Passover celebration, when His parents left and went back toward Nazareth, their hometown, it took them a while to realize that Jesus was not with them. His parents had assumed that Jesus had mixed in the crowd of people returning home after the festival. After a day's journey, His parents looked for Jesus and did not find Him. They went back to Jerusalem, searching for Him. After three days, they found Him in the temple, sitting among the teachers of the law, listening to them and asking them questions.

> "When his parents saw him they were astonished; and his mother said to him, 'Child, why have you treated us like this? Look, your father and I have been searching for you in great anxiety.' He said to them, 'Why were you searching for me? Did you not know that I must be in my Father's house?'" (Luke 2:48–49).

At the age of thirty, after committing His life to follow the will of God, Jesus went to the wilderness to clarify His life's purpose and bring it into the purpose of God. He was giving control over to the new file, allowing it to overwrite all the other files. Jesus took forty days and forty nights alone in the wilderness to define and focus on His purpose in life. He sought the heart of God and allowed the Spirit of God to have control over His inner being: the triangles. Applying the new file over the old files was an intense learning process; Jesus had to choose God's Spirit over self-desire and give up control to God's love to balance the triangles. The ultimate test came in the form of temptation. Jesus did not allow His old files to control Him; rather, He allowed the new file to guide Him. Jesus came out of the wilderness with a clear picture of His mission. His mission statement was also the purpose statement for His life: "The Spirit of the Lord is upon me, because he has anointed me to bring good news to the poor. He has sent me to proclaim release to the captives and recovery of sight to the blind, to let the oppressed go free, to proclaim the year of the Lord's favor" (Luke 4:18–19).

Jesus declared His mission as the purpose statement of His life, and He carried out that mission as His life's vocation. He did not seek shortcuts to do His mission at the expense of His relationship with the Spirit of the heavenly Father. The temptations he faced were meant to quicken His mission using shortcuts. Jesus did not allow the members of the triangles to take control but fully submitted to the Spirit of God. He did not succumb to the needs of His body and the subsequent prompting of the members of the angles to take the lead but instead listened to the Spirit of God. Through this submission, He applied the new file and a new way of living. He did not live by the standard of the world but by the standard of God's Spirit, divine love.

Jesus's teachings challenged His followers to set a new standard of living. He pointed out that murder is not only a physical action but also an emotional one: "You have heard that it was said to those of ancient times, 'You shall not murder'; and 'whoever murders shall be liable to judgment.' But I say to you that if you are angry with a brother or sister, you will be liable to judgment; and if you insult a brother or sister, you will be liable to the council; and if you say, 'You fool,' you will be liable to the hell of fire" (Matthew 5:21–22).

In the same discourse, Jesus pointed out that adultery is not only a physical action but also an action of the mind: "You have heard that it was said, 'You shall not commit adultery.' But I say to you that everyone who looks at a woman with lust has already committed adultery with her in his heart" (vv. 27–28).

Paul, the apostle of Jesus Christ, declared his experience:

"So I find it to be a law that when I want to do what is good, evil lies close at hand. For I delight in the law of God in my inmost self, but I see in my members another law at war with the law of my mind, making me captive to the law of sin that dwells in my members. Wretched man that I am! Who will rescue me from this body of death? Thanks be to God through Jesus Christ our Lord!" (Romans 7:21–25).

Therefore, the Apostle Paul made a commitment: ". . . I have been crucified with Christ; and it is no longer I who live, but it is Christ who lives in me. And the life I now live in the flesh I live by faith in the Son of God, who loved me and gave himself for me" (Galatians 2:19–21).

This is the testimony of the complete submission of the inner being, the cravings of the body, and the prompting of all members of the triangles to follow the will of God. It is both submission to the inner triangle—made of the Father, Son, and Holy Spirit—and drawing energy from that creative source.

The third step to spiritual discipline is carrying out the mission—the purpose for life—and enjoying the fullness of life. Jesus announced God's good news to the poor. He gave hope to the hopeless, healing to the sick, and dignity to the destitute. He gave a greater vision of the kingdom of God to all His followers. Jesus said, "The thief comes only to steal and kill and destroy. I came that they may have life, and have it abundantly" (John 10:10).

Health, wealth, and prosperity in life are not evil. When we integrate our purpose with the purpose of God, however, these things will not become the goal of our lives. Submitting to God's Spirit will bring the best out of all situations in life. The right uses of health, wealth, and prosperity will become routine. Jesus taught that worry is caused by lack of trust in God. People who do not place God first in their lives, submitting everything to the guidance of God's Spirit, are subject to worry. Those who set God first in their lives and allow the Spirit of God to take control of everything else will enjoy the fullness of life. Jesus said, "But strive first for the kingdom of God and his righteousness, and all these things will be given to you as well" (Matthew 6:33).

The Apostle Paul said, "I know what it is to be in need, and I know what it is to have plenty. I have learned the secret of being content in any and every situation, whether well fed or hungry, whether living in plenty or in want. I can do all this through him who gives me strength" (Philippians 4:12–13, NIV).

Giving control to the Spirit of God is being in Christ. It is practicing self-discipline and being online with God, enjoying the fullness of life as the Creator intended.

STUDY QUESTIONS

1. What are the three tiers of influence?

2. What is the main objective of the natural mind?

3. Do Christians need to isolate themselves from the world to practice self-denial?

4. What does it mean "to be crucified with Christ"?

5. How can one practice spiritual discipline?

CHAPTER

7

CREATING A NEW WORLD

God created the three-dimensional world in which we live. God created three planes of existence in this order: spiritual world, internal world, and external world.

First, in the beginning was God. Second, God's Spirit was moving and acting. Third, the world came into existence. Most people, however, view the world in a different order. They see first the external world, then the internal world, and lastly, the spiritual world. Therefore, those people prioritize creating a better external world full of material things that bring physical comfort. Most of the time, they create an internal world with the knowledge for acquiring material things that provide physical comfort and security. Lastly, they seek God's help to meet their spiritual needs. A good percentage of Christian people seek God's help, not to create a better spiritual world, but a better physical one. Jesus challenged His followers to rearrange their priorities by placing spiritual needs first:

> "Therefore do not worry, saying, 'What will we eat?' or 'What will we drink?' or 'What will we wear?' For it is the Gentiles who strive for all these things; and indeed your heavenly Father knows that you need all these things. But strive first for the kingdom of God and his righteousness, and all these things will be given to you as well" (Matthew 6:31–33).

The human spirit must reach out to the Spirit of God to participate in the resources of the creative energy. This should be the number one priority in the order of the new creation. When we reach out to the Spirit of God, we are obedient, allowing the Spirit of God to balance all the triangles of our inner beings. In this process, the members of the triangles are not only balanced but also empowered. When our triangles are balanced, we live in harmony with God's Spirit and can build a better world with the help of God's creative energy. This is living online with God.

Being online with God is actively participating in God's creative energy. With the creative energy of God, we can recreate a new internal world, which will help us to create a new external world. Participating in God's creative energy allows the creative resources of our inner triangles to help create better outer triangles.

When all the triangles are controlled and empowered by the Spirit of God, members of the triangles will not act without the consent of all members. The Spirit of God will guide members of the triangles to work together without creating conflict with one another and producing destructive energy. Under the guidance of God's Spirit, the triangles work together, participating with the creative energy to produce a new and better world.

CREATING A SPIRITUAL WORLD

Jesus, the Master Teacher, taught:

> "Either make the tree good, and its fruit good; or make the tree bad, and its fruit bad; for the tree is known by its fruit. You brood of vipers! How can you speak good things, when you are evil? For out of the abundance of the heart the mouth speaks. The good person

brings good things out of a good treasure, and the evil person brings evil things out of an evil treasure. I tell you, on the day of judgment you will have to give an account for every careless word you utter; for by your words you will be justified, and by your words you will be condemned" (Matthew 12:33–37).

Jesus was not talking about literal trees; He was comparing human beings to trees. A tree is identified by its fruit. The fruit of the tree is a product of what is within the tree. Grafting is the age-old practice of making trees produce better-tasting and higher quantities of fruit than they can on their own. Grafting is to take the bud of a desirable, good, and productive tree and attach it to a natural tree that either produces bad fruit or does not produce at all. When the new bud starts growing, the natural tree is cut away to divert resources to the graft, allowing the new bud to grow and produce the desired fruit.

Imagine two trees. One is a native and non-producing persimmon tree grafted with scion buds (the small branch used for grafting) of a producing Japanese persimmon tree. It had seven branches, and each one of them was grafted. However, only one branch accepted the grafted bud and grew. The other tree is a grafted and producing Fuyu persimmon tree. "Unlike the cultivated persimmon, the wild persimmon varieties are small and very astringent until completely ripe. They are usually ripe after the first frost and all the leaves have fallen from the tree, though even then some fruit can still be very astringent."[20]

Native persimmons leave an undesirable, dry, astringent aftertaste for many hours. However, the grafted Fuyu persimmon fruit is delicious to eat, lacking that astringent aftertaste, and it has many health benefits.

I grew up in the most southern and tropical part of India. I had great affection for trees and was privileged to live in a coconut grove filled with varieties of tropical evergreens. During my adolescent years, rubber trees replaced coconut palms, cashew trees, and black pepper vines as cash crops. Farmers planted rubber seedlings and cultivated them for five years to tap their latex. Soon, grafting was introduced to enhance production. One morning, I walked to school through our small rubber plantation. The trees grew vigorously in the tropical sun during the latter part of the monsoon season. Late that afternoon, when I walked back from school, I was saddened by the devastation of the rubber grove. All the trees had been cut down, like a mighty army beheaded by enemy soldiers, with a scattered few still alive to tell the terrible story.

The trees that accepted the grafted shoots were cut down to give life to the new shoot. They experienced the pain of death to their old selves, followed by the power of resurrection in their newly grafted buds. The few trees scattered around the plantation did not suffer the pain of death because they did not accept the grafted bud. When harvested, the grafted trees produced greater amounts of liquid rubber than the natural trees. However, some farmers, afraid of cutting down their natural trees, did not graft their crops. It was a costly lesson for those farmers.

Grafting and pruning were familiar lessons to Jesus's audience. These horticultural principles apply to spiritual principles for human behavior. Jesus said:

> "I am the true vine, and my Father is the vinegrower. He removes every branch in me that bears no fruit. Every branch that bears fruit he prunes to make it bear more fruit. You have already been cleansed by the word that I have spoken to you. Abide in me as I abide in you. Just as the branch cannot bear fruit by itself unless it abides in the vine, neither can you unless you abide in me. I am the vine; you are the branches. Those who abide in me and I in them bear much

fruit, because apart from me you can do nothing. Whoever does not abide in me is thrown away like a branch and withers; such branches are gathered, thrown into the fire, and burned. If you abide in me, and my words abide in you, ask for whatever you wish, and it will be done for you. My Father is glorified by this, that you bear much fruit and become my disciples. As the Father has loved me, so I have loved you; abide in my love. If you keep my commandments, you will abide in my love, just as I have kept my Father's commandments and abide in his love. I have said these things to you so that my joy may be in you, and that your joy may be complete.

This is my commandment, that you love one another as I have loved you. No one has greater love than this, to lay down one's life for one's friends. You are my friends if you do what I command you. I do not call you servants any longer, because the servant does not know what the master is doing; but I have called you friends, because I have made known to you everything that I have heard from my Father. You did not choose me but I chose you. And I appointed you to go and bear fruit, fruit that will last, so that the Father will give you whatever you ask him in my name. I am giving you these commands so that you may love one another" (John 15:1–17).

Jesus did not teach an impractical principle but a very practical one. The natural tree represents Adam and Eve, who were not submissive to or controlled by God's Spirit but were instead controlled by the members of the triangles and without the Spirit of God. Those members represented files of information controlled by the body's (flesh and blood) need and desire without the guidance of the Spirit of God. The natural tree, without the internal influence of the Spirit of God, produces bad fruit. "Now the works of the flesh are obvious: fornication, impurity, licentiousness, idolatry, sorcery, enmities, strife, jealousy, anger, quarrels, dissensions, factions, envy, drunkenness, carousing, and things like these. I am warning you, as I warned you before: those who do such things will not inherit the kingdom of God" (Galatians 5:19–21).

The natural tree grows and thrives by living in the natural world. It has a strong root system that penetrates the soil, and it grows in the native soil without needing much care from the grower. Yet it produces no good fruit. Its fruit contains poisonous and destructive elements. This is like anger producing revenge, and revenge pursuing retaliation. Selfish ambition seeks self-fulfillment without the consideration of others. The natural tendencies of our personality traits create conflict within and produce unhealthy relationships. Negative factors—guilt, shame, pride, arrogance, self-pity, greed, jealousy—must be cut off to give strength and power to the Spirit of God to lead and guide the internal process for healthy and wholesome relationships and action.

The grafted tree represents the person who submits to God's Spirit and allows that Spirit to control the members of their triangles. Just like a grafted tree grows a new shoot, a person who allows the Spirit of God to take control of their life must work against the natural influences of the flesh and blood. They live in harmony with the Spirit of God and balance the angles of the triangles. The grafted tree, empowered by the creative energy of God, produces good fruit. "By contrast, the fruit of the Spirit is love, joy, peace, patience, kindness, generosity, faithfulness, gentleness, and self-control. There is no law against such things. And those who belong to Christ Jesus have crucified the flesh with its passions and desires. If we live by the Spirit, let us also be guided by the Spirit" (Galatians 5:22–25).

Most people, especially Christians, do not see themselves represented in the natural tree. Therefore, a carnal person, represented by the natural tree, uses the information in the mind and modifies their behavior accordingly.

She is controlled by the self-interest of her mind rather than being controlled by the love of God. Therefore, she returns love for love and hate for hate. The natural objective of her mind is to use information for her own benefit. She does not practice redemptive love. She does not look out for others' interests, but her own. At best, her attitude is like that of a merchant who keeps the customer happy to retain the customer's business. At worst, her attitude is like that of a merchant seeking profits at the expense of the customer.

A Christian, representing the grafted tree, uses the Spirit of Christ to dictate her behavior. Her aim is not only to have acceptable behavior, but to also practice redemptive love. She is not only looking out for her interests but also for the interests of others. She does not use others for self-gain and does not seek benefits at the expense of others. On the contrary, she seeks to bless others. She lives with a mission for her life and seeks for the Spirit of Christ to control her life. She lives in harmony with the Spirit of God.

Natural tendencies are not completely removed from the grafted tree. Its roots and basic stems always remain natural, and they exercise the power to produce fruit. The Christian representing the grafted bud must be on guard to subdue the power of the natural elements. The Apostle Paul testified: ". . . I have been crucified with Christ; and it is no longer I who live, but it is Christ who lives in me. And the life I now live in the flesh I live by faith in the Son of God, who loved me and gave himself for me" (Galatians 2:19–20).

The Apostle Paul also said that he died daily. He confirmed the fact that, even though he experienced spiritual grafting, he must continue to choose his spiritual nature over the carnal nature. The new files must overwrite the old files. The old files are not removed; they are still in the computer. The natural tendencies lay dormant in the subconscious mind but seek opportunities to exercise power over the spiritual nature. Keeping the power of the old nature submissive to the new nature is to experience death. The pain of this death depends on the intensity of the desires of the old nature.

The good news is that, by allowing the grafted bud to grow, the tree becomes new. Through the practice of overwriting our natural tendencies, the spiritual mind grows and becomes stronger. By applying the Word of God at the conception of a thought and transcending to the Spirit of God, the human mind will draw spiritual energy from the Creator. In this process, spiritual discipline becomes the way of life for those who are controlled by the Spirit of God. They live online with God. They are in God, and God is in them. Their innermost beings—the members of the triangles—are alive and active, working together in harmony. Their thoughts are centered on God, and they meditate on God's goodness. Their hearts are full of love, and nothing can separate them from God's love. Those controlled by the Spirit of God are the participants of the kingdom of God. The evils of the world cannot negatively influence or destroy them. On the contrary, with the creative energy of God's love within them, they recreate their external world. They live in the Spirit of God and enjoy the presence of God, just as Adam and Eve experienced it in the garden of Eden prior to their disobedience. In the Spirit, people walk and talk with God as their friend and companion. They live with praise and thanksgiving to God in their inner beings. They are indeed the salt of the earth and light of the world. Their words, attitudes, and actions touch others with the touch of God.

CREATING AN INTERNAL WORLD

The first step in recreating the internal world is to correctly apply the creative energy within the inner triangles. At the beginning of creation, the universe was like a blob. There was no order. The Spirit of God hovered over the blob. "Then God said, 'Let there be light'; and there was light. And God saw that the light was good; and God separated the light from the darkness. God called the light Day, and the darkness he called Night. And there was evening and there was morning, the first day" (Genesis 1:3–5).

The phrase, "Then God said," is the key. The Word of God is the key to creation, which brought order out of chaos. It is the Word of God that brought something out of nothing, and it is the power of God that creates and recreates a human's inner being. The Word of God is not only the power of God at the time of creation but also the agent by which God makes His will known to us. Jesus was the visible manifestation of the Word of God: "In the beginning was the Word, and the Word was with God, and the Word was God. He was with God in the beginning. Through him all things were made; without him nothing was made that has been made. In him was life, and that life was the light of all mankind. The light shines in the darkness, and the darkness has not overcome it" (John 1:1–5).

Jesus was God in action. The Spirit that manifested through Jesus of Nazareth is the Spirit of God, who can recreate us in the image of God. The Apostle Paul highlighted God's Spirit as the mystery hidden for generations, finally disclosed to the saints. To participate in the Spirit of Christ is to participate in the creative energy of God. Abiding in Christ is being plugged into the Spirit of God, as Christ abided in the Spirit of the heavenly Father. To abide in Christ is to connect with the Spirit of God, using the creative energy of God to create a new world.

In this new world is a new order. The old world order said: "Love your neighbor and hate your enemy." The new world order says: "Love your enemies and pray for those who persecute you" (Matthew 5:44). The old world order said: "Do not murder; anyone who murders will be subject to judgment." The new world order says: "Anyone who is angry with his brother or sister will be subject to judgment" (Matthew 5:22, NIV). In the new world order, every thought is filtered through the Spirit of Christ to work with the Spirit of God. Removing thoughts that are not in harmony with the Spirit of God is like pruning a bush. We must use a master disk to cancel out our thoughts that are prompted by the old world order. We are called to process our thoughts through the Spirit of Christ and act on behalf of God. The author of the book of Hebrews wrote, "Indeed, the word of God is living and active, sharper than any two-edged sword, piercing until it divides soul from spirit, joints from marrow; it is able to judge the thoughts and intentions of the heart. And before him no creature is hidden, but all are naked and laid bare to the eyes of the one to whom we must render an account" (Hebrews 4:12–13).

Most people possess a mixture of good and bad tendencies. Most Christians have good intentions of being good people. They are not any different from non-Christians who have good intentions of being good people. Intentions alone do not create a new world. Intentions are subject to the information stored up in our minds. People act good or bad depending upon the circumstances and situations of life. They live in a neutral zone, neither hot nor cold. Their external worlds exercise control over their internal worlds. Intentions must become commitments of the mind, and the mind must follow the Spirit of God to act on those good intentions.

The conception of action begins with thought. It is thought—a member of the third triangle—that prompts our minds for the process of action. Thought is the subtle force that penetrates between the soul and the spirit, giving life and processing information into action. The soul is like the electricity that gives life to the computer, and thought is the byte of information, the prime mover of the mind. The existing information in the mind associates with incoming information and produces both attitudes and actions. If our minds are not formatted with the Spirit of Christ, they will produce the attitudes and actions of the old nature. However, if our minds are trained to filter information to work with the Spirit of Christ, they will yield to God's Spirit for attitudes and actions. When our minds yield to the Spirit of God, thought is processed to act with spiritual tendencies, not with natural tendencies. The Spirit of God enables us to use the information of our minds in the most effective way for the best results. In this process, our minds and spirits do not work independently of each other—they work together. The difference is that we do not only apply the knowledge of our minds but also use the guidance of God's Spirit for action. We not only do a job; we care about how the job is done and how it may affect our lives and the lives of others.

(Body, Soul, and Spirit) Thoughts (Natural Mind)

=

Attitude and Action Benefitting Self

(Body, Soul, and Spirit) Thoughts (Grafted Mind)

=

Attitude and Action Benefitting Self and Others

The body produces some thoughts for physical wellbeing, such as hunger and thirst. Thoughts are generated by one's need for rest and recreation, feelings of leisure and pleasure, drive for physical attraction and sex, desire for security and fear of death, care for one's family, and relationship with the immediate and wider world. These and many other factors produce thoughts. There is built-in (innate) and stored (learned) information in the mind that associates with the incoming thought (new information) and processes it for action.

The human condition of the Adam (old) nature is to act on behalf of the natural body and its demands. The old nature makes decisions without God, rebelling against or ignoring God's Word in the process. Like computer software programmed to work with a master file, the mind works with the incoming thoughts—either with the old nature or with the new nature—as a master file of the mind. Jesus pointed out that the good man brings good things out of the good stored up in him and the evil man brings evil things out of the evil stored up in him: "For out of the heart come evil intentions, murder, adultery, fornication, theft, false witness, slander" (Matthew 15:19). Therefore, the stored information of the mind must be harmonious to work with the Spirit of God. The new nature, formatted by the Spirit of Christ, brings thoughts into submission to the Word of God. In this process, our world is not created by the needs and desires of the flesh and blood, but by the Spirit of the Creator.

> "For those who live according to the flesh set their minds on the things of the flesh, but those who live according to the Spirit set their minds on the things of the Spirit. To set the mind on the flesh is death, but to set the mind on the Spirit is life and peace. For this reason the mind that is set on the flesh is hostile to God; it does not submit to God's law—indeed it cannot, and those who are in the flesh cannot please God. But you are not in the flesh; you are in the Spirit, since the Spirit of God dwells in you. Anyone who does not have the Spirit of Christ does not belong to him" (Romans 8:5–9).

When we do not allow the Spirit of God to control our thoughts, we allow the old nature to control us. Prolonged resistance of God's Spirit makes our attitudes and actions chronically self-centered: we partake in stubbornness, prejudice, hate, self-righteousness, greed, lust, and other forms of self-gratifying behavior. Uncontrolled natural thoughts, born of the body's needs and desires, allow the old self to take control of the information of the mind without restraint. Uncontrolled natural thoughts use the carnal nature of the old self without yielding to God's Spirit. In this process, carnal imaginations hover over the mind, just as the Spirit of God hovered over the chaos at the beginning of creation. The result is that the evil imagination produces evil actions. Attitudes and actions produce pain and suffering in the world. "The Lord saw that the wickedness of humankind was great in the earth, and that *every inclination of the thoughts of their hearts was only evil continually*" (Genesis 6:5, emphasis mine).

Carnally-minded people participate in evil imaginations and produce carnal actions. They join with the destructive forces in creating an evil world.

Spiritually-minded people participate in good thoughts and produce wholesome actions. They join forces with the creative power of God in creating a good world. At His temptations, Jesus did not join destructive forces; He joined the creative forces. He was meditating on God's Word, and the Spirit of God hovered over His mind. Therefore, Jesus could discern the will of God for the right response. In response to His temptation of turning the stones into bread, Jesus answered: "It is written, 'One does not live by bread alone, but by *every word that comes from the mouth of God*'" (Matthew 4:4, emphasis mine).

Jesus did not allow His thought, prompted by hunger, to associate with destructive forces and challenge the integrity of God. Thought penetrated between the soul and the spirit. Before thought could prompt the stored information in the mind for action, Jesus used the Word of God to override the natural thought of the old self. In this process, Jesus not only subdued the power of the old nature but also created a new world order.

The old world order demanded physical food to satisfy physical hunger. Jesus pointed out that physical food alone would not satisfy the hunger of human beings. We are different from all other creatures. Natural food can stop our physical hunger, but it can also hurt our entire being. Therefore, how we obtain natural food should be in harmony with the Spirit of God. If we seek satisfaction through natural food alone, we are no better than the beasts of the wild. "Jesus said to them, '*My food is to do the will of him who sent me and to complete his work*'" (John 4:34, emphasis mine). Jesus's mission and purpose for life was to do the will of God. His pain of hunger, caused by forty days of fasting, could change His thought. The subtle question of the temptation did not appear as a negative challenge to God's integrity, but as a positive affirmation of God's faithfulness. Jesus discerned the difference by bringing His triangles into harmony with the Spirit of God. His submission to God's Spirit brought all angles of His triangles into balance. He was energized even without physical food. Jesus's inner being—the triangles—worked together and created a new order of priority and a new internal world.

CREATING AN EXTERNAL WORLD

(Body, Soul, and Spirit) Thoughts (Natural Mind)

=

Attitude and Action from the Natural Mind

=

Self-Centered Words, or Words Ultimately for the Benefit of the Self

(Body, Soul and Spirit) Thoughts (Grafted Mind)

=

Attitude and Action Guided by the Spirit of God

=

Wholesome Words, or Words Benefitting the Self and Others

Thought initiates the internal process for action. Thought sends information to the mind, and the mind sends it to the members of the triangles, with or without the guidance of the Spirit of God for action. The Word of God should guide the spirit of a child of God. It is the Word of God that—as the creative energy of God—interacts with the human spirit. Jesus Christ is the visible manifestation of the Word of God. Jesus stands as the perfect example of complete obedience to the Spirit of God. The Word of God is revealed to us through the words of God, the Scriptures: "I treasure your word in my heart, so that I may not sin against you" (Psalm 119:11).

Our spoken words reveal the controlling thoughts of our mind. The psalmist confessed, "Even before a word is on my tongue O Lord, you know it completely" (Psalm 139:4).

Thoughts in our inner beings prompt spoken words, which have the power to create or destroy. Spoken words reveal the true nature of our inner beings. "And we speak of these things in words not taught by human wisdom but taught by the Spirit, interpreting spiritual things to those who are spiritual" (1 Corinthians 2:13).

Remember the teachings of the Master Teacher:

". . . For out of the abundance of the heart the mouth speaks. The good person brings good things out of a good treasure, and the evil person brings evil things out of an evil treasure. I tell you, on the day of judgment you will have to give an account for every careless word you utter; for by your words you will be justified, and by your words you will be condemned" (Matthew 12:34–37).

When our words are guided by God's Spirit, they become manifestations of love: patient and kind. Godly words have the power to change our situations and circumstances. God's words have the power to create newness out of the old. God's word has the power to heal: "He sent out *his word* and healed them, and delivered them from destruction" (Psalm 107:20, emphasis mine). Therefore, we can create a new order around us and overcome the negative forces that try to control us.

Having control over our thoughts gives us control over our words. Those who rely on the old self—Adam's nature—process thoughts into self-centered words. Those who do not process their thoughts will fail to control their tongues. Those who process their thoughts through the Spirit of Christ speak words of life. The Bible tells us that God created the universe by His words: "*Then God said*, 'Let there be light'; and there was light" (Genesis 1:3, emphasis mine).

EXAMPLES

A husband and wife prepared for a summer vacation with their teenage daughter. It was not just a vacation, but an opportunity to check out major universities their daughter might attend for college. An Ivy League university announced their summer programs, and the father found a weeklong course for his continuing education. At the same time, there were mini programs that the mother and daughter could attend. In addition to the great educational opportunity, recreational programs also were available to the family. The family took advantage of these great opportunities. They registered three months early and looked forward to the weeklong event on the East Coast.

When the day came to leave, they were happy to fly from Dallas to New York. They rented a car in the city and drove to the historical university. Friendly and hospitable staff greeted them and took them to the dormitory furnished for visiting families. The building reminded the parents of their college days, but it was the first time their daughter had ever been inside a college dorm.

After leaving their luggage in the dorm, the family toured the university's campus to get acquainted with its many buildings. When the tour was over, they ate a good dinner in the cafeteria and attended a general assembly for all new guests.

Everything moved along as planned until that evening. The teenage daughter had gone ahead of her parents to take a shower at the dorm but quickly returned. She told her parents that she could not enter the bathroom because it was occupied and there was a long line of people waiting. In disbelief, her father went to check out the situation.

The men's restroom was locked because of a major leak, so both men and women had to use the one bathroom designated for women. The OCCUPIED sign was an inadequate solution since only one person could enter the bathroom at a time, although there were several showers and lavatories that could accommodate multiple people.

The father, a minister, had the choice of joining the complainers standing in line, or seek ways to change the situation. Since many of the others in line were ministers with their children, a call to prayer did not make good sense to him. He considered telling some jokes that might reduce the tension. He thought, '*I have the power within me to change the situation for the better or for the worse. Yes, I can create my internal world, as well as my external world, and invite others to enter it.*' But could he make it happen? How could he create a new external world with the change of the new internal world?

In his internal world, he could empathize with the hosts at the university. They had prepared many nice things for their guests, but one bad incident made the whole situation seem untenable. As he pondered how to change the situation, another thought went through his mind: '*If I were the host, what would I do to make the situation a pleasant one?*' He ran to his room, took a sheet of paper, and wrote "MEN" on one side and "WOMEN" on the other. He went to the head of the line and asked those who stood at the door whether there was a man or a woman in the bathroom. They said woman, so he placed the "WOMEN" side of the sign on the door and motioned for other women to go in. About half a dozen of the women in line rushed into the restroom, thanking the man as they passed him. When the last woman came out, she changed the sign to the "MEN" side. The men could then go in and take care of their personal needs.

Let me provide another example of influencing the external world with the power of the spiritual and internal world.

One Sunday morning, congregants participated in a very dignified formal worship service, as usual. Most of the worshippers were in their sixties, seventies, or older. No child had been born to any of the members for over twenty years. If visitors or family members came to the worship service with children in tow, they had to follow two unwritten rules: "Do not disturb the older congregants" and "Do not let your children cry when the preacher is speaking."

The church had invited a new, young, student minister to be their pastor. He reached out to the community and invited all kinds of people, including a young couple with two children. One child was a toddler, and the other was an infant. The new pastor, aware of their presence, thanked God in his heart for the visiting couple with children. In an informal moment of friendship, he apologized to the couple for the church's lack of a nursery. He prayed in his heart that the children would behave well so that everyone in the church would be happy to have their guests in worship.

The inevitable happened. As he preached, the baby began to cry loudly. The mother, hoping the child would stop, did not leave the sanctuary. The minister, sensing the couple's discomfort and the congregation's tension, said, "I thank God for the cry of a child in this place. How long has it been since we heard a cry of a child in this place?"

"Too long," a man responded from the back pew.

The minister continued, addressing the visiting couple: "I thank God that you came today with your children. It is a new beginning for us as a church. The cry is not disturbing me, and I believe it is not disturbing you or anyone else. I would rather hear a child cry here in worship than have no child at all in this place."

His words elicited applause, but he did not stop preaching. "Jesus said, 'Unless you become like a child, you cannot enter the kingdom of God.' You do not tell your children not to come to you because they cry, do you? When they cry, what you would do? You reach out to carry them in your arms; you try to talk to them in a way they understand. We become like children when we talk to our children. We bend down, listen to them, and talk to them softly and gently."

The worship service continued with great joy and affirmation of the young couple and their children. Perhaps it was the applause, the gentle tone of the minister, the bottle the mother gave to the baby, or the direct intervention of God, but the little child became quiet and went to sleep in the arms of its mother.

When the worship was over, a line of older folks—grandparents and great-grandparents—wanted to hold the little children in their arms. Some of them bent down and talked to the toddler just as they talked to their grandchildren or great-grandchildren. A family invited the couple and their children to lunch in their home. The older church found a new beginning, a new vision, and a new enthusiasm. Within the next few months, new families with children joined the church for worship. Each Sunday during worship, they had a "children's moment." Within four years, this church had many younger people in its worship services.

Search your heart and let the Spirit of God take charge. Use the Spirit of God within you to create first a new internal world, and then a new external world.

The new external world often begins with the words you use. God revealed His nature and purpose to people through the spoken word: "*So shall my word* be that goes out from my mouth; it shall not return to me empty, but it shall accomplish that which I purpose, and succeed in the thing for which I sent it" (Isaiah 55:11, emphasis mine).

The prophets uttered God's Word by saying either "the word of the Lord," "thus says the Lord," or "hear the word of the Lord" to proclaim the message of God.

Blessings and curses were passed on to people through the spoken word. Isaac could not change his words of blessing he uttered to his son Jacob, even though Isaac thought he was blessing Esau. At times, spoken words were associated with magical power for action. Kings sought words of wisdom from wise people. Kings of Israel sought God's words from the prophets. The prophet Jeremiah was imprisoned for uttering discouraging words. False prophets uttered pleasing words in the name of God but lacked integrity. Only true prophets could speak the true message of God:

> "Then Balak's anger was kindled against Balaam, and he struck his hands together. Balak said to Balaam, 'I summoned you to curse my enemies, but instead you have blessed them these three times. Now be off with you! Go home! I said, "I will reward you

richly," but the Lord has denied you any reward.' And Balaam said to Balak, 'Did I not tell your messengers whom you sent to me, "If Balak should give me his house full of silver and gold, I would not be able to go beyond the word of the Lord, to do either good or bad of my own will; what the Lord says, that is what I will say"?'" (Numbers 24:10–13).

PSYCHOLOGICAL EFFECT OF SPOKEN WORDS

The words we speak and the words we hear prompt the thought processes of our minds. Words come out of the thoughts from the mind and activate images to represent the words. Thus, words affect the one who speaks just as much as the one who hears. Words can provoke love or hate, apathy or action, holiness or lust, peace or anger, encouragement or discouragement. Spoken words and their influence can be grouped into three categories: negative, neutral, and positive.

1. NEGATIVE USE OF WORDS

The negative group of words comes out of the old nature. This group represents the bad tree that produces bad fruit and the old disk of unholy imagery that do not submit to God's Spirit. The Apostle James wrote the following:

"Or look at ships: though they are so large that it takes strong winds to drive them, yet they are guided by a very small rudder wherever the will of the pilot directs. So also the tongue is a small member, yet it boasts of great exploits. How great a forest is set ablaze by a small fire! And the tongue is a fire. The tongue is placed among our members as a world of iniquity; it stains the whole body, sets on fire the cycle of nature, and is itself set on fire by hell" (James 3:4–6).

The tongue is an instrument of the mind. Through spoken words, the tongue reveals the nature of the mind. In spoken words, we use internal energy to create the external world. Words of profanity create an unholy atmosphere. Hateful words break up relationships and create a world of hostility. Words of discouragement create a pessimistic world. Using negative words, we become the agent of the Evil One, Satan the destroyer.

Words are building blocks. When we use good words, we reveal our inner thoughts—good thoughts—and invite others to join in the building up of a good world. In the same way, when we use curse words, we invite the cursed person to join a bad world. The corrupted mind speaks words that are corrupted by the old nature. The angles of the triangles are not balanced. They try to overcome evil by the force of evil.

Jesus taught that we are not to return evil for evil. Responding to evil words with more evil words only builds up an evil world. Responding to evil with evil merely plays into the hands of the evil person. As a spiritual discipline, we should first evaluate our words: Are my words building blocks for a good world or an evil world? Second, we should forgive others who use evil words. By forgiving others, we remove the negative building blocks from our minds. Otherwise, we could allow negative thought—prompted by the negative words—to make negative associations in our minds and, thus, unbalance the triangles within our inner beings.

2. NEUTRAL USE OF WORDS

The neutral group of words is neither positive nor negative. The neutral group may give the appearance of being positive or negative without entirely associating with one or the other. People who use neutral words live with both good and bad; they use these words as situations dictate. The Apostle James asked us to examine the neutrality of the tongue:

> "With it we bless the Lord and Father, and with it we curse those who are made in the likeness of God. From the same mouth come blessing and cursing. My brothers and sisters, this ought not to be so. Does a spring pour forth from the same opening both fresh and brackish water? Can a fig tree, my brothers and sisters, yield olives, or a grapevine figs? No more can saltwater yield fresh" (James 3:9–12).

Most Christians live in this neutral zone. They do not use bad words all the time and they do not use good words all the time. However, they are not always careful about how they speak. Jesus said, "I tell you, on the day of judgment you will have to give an account for every careless word you utter; for by your words you will be justified, and by your words you will be condemned" (Matthew 12:36–37).

It may sound harsh and impractical, but remember that the Apostle Paul taught that there is no condemnation for those who are in Christ Jesus, who do not live according to the sinful nature but according to the Spirit. Neutral Christians often fall into the camp of the negative people. Spiritual discipline helps them to move from using negative words to positive words. Daily examination of the words we use and the thoughts that prompt the use of such words will help us reduce the use of negative words. The psalmist David knew the importance of using the right words and having the right thoughts. He prayed: "Set a guard over my mouth, O Lord; keep watch over the door of my lips. Do not turn my heart to any evil, to busy myself with wicked deeds in company with those who work iniquity; do not let me eat of their delicacies" (Psalm 141:3–4) and "Search me, O God, and know my heart; test me and know my thoughts. See if there is any wicked way in me, and lead me in the way everlasting" (Psalm 139:23–24).

3. POSITIVE USE OF WORDS

The former football coach of the Dallas Cowboys, the late Tom Landry, used to say that "a good offense is the best defense." A good offense is using a positive and creative group of words. To find and use positive and creative words, we must meditate on God's goodness. The psalmist David confronted evil attacks, and he testified that trusting and praising God is a positive and offensive weapon against the use of negative words: "Be gracious to me, O God, for people trample on me; all day long foes oppress me; my enemies trample on me all day long, for many fight against me. O Most High, when I am afraid, I put my trust in you. In God, whose word I praise, in God I trust; I am not afraid; what can flesh do to me?" (Psalm 56:1–4).

When we trust and praise God, our thoughts are God-centered, which in turn centers our triangles to work in harmony and produce creative energy. Trusting God connects the mortal spirit with the divine Spirit. It is being online with God. When we trust God, we can praise God for His goodness. The psalmist said, "I have been like a portent to many, but you are my strong refuge. My mouth is filled with your praise, and with your glory all day long" (Psalm 71:7–8).

David understood the spiritual principles of using positive and creative words. He practiced positive speaking by praising God. When our minds are filled with praise and thanksgiving to God, the positive power of God's Word connects with our minds. It is the experience of God incarnating within our inner beings. This positive power then flows into the inner triangle—the mind—and invites the Spirit of God to dwell in the center and control all the members of the triangles. The inner triangle of God's creative power empowers the outer triangles and enables our minds to make positive responses. In this state, we no longer speak under the influence of the old file, but under the influence of the new file. Therefore, our spoken words are filled with creative power. They are words that create love, joy, peace, patience, kindness, goodness, faithfulness, gentleness, and self-control. We can then speak words of encouragement against discouragement, hope against despair, healing against hurt, and peace against trouble. We become God's agents of reconciliation.

When we abide in Christ and praise God, we become a partner in the Spirit of Christ. Jesus said, "On that day you will know that I am in my Father, and you in me, and I in you" (John 14:20).

Christians often fail to believe in and act on the Word of God. Some of them are even afraid to regularly practice spiritual principles, thinking that they might become too religious and miss all the fun the world offers. They then fail to enjoy the fullness of God's Spirit and power. The truth is, practicing spiritual principles allows us to enjoy life more abundantly.

Practicing spiritual disciplines allows the Spirit of God to guide our thought processes that lead to action. Regularly practicing spiritual disciplines conditions the members of the triangles to work together in harmony. It helps the mind to regulate and automate responses to the external world through the Spirit of Christ.

STUDY QUESTIONS

1. What is the three-dimensional world?

2. What is the practical reality of being grafted with Christ?

3. The Apostle Paul said that he died daily. Do you have to die daily? If so, how?

4. What is the importance of spoken words?

5. How do you create your new world?

CHAPTER
8

Living in the New World

There are three levels of living standards. The first level is living in the world as friends of the world. At this level, people produce the fruit of the natural tree. They do not submit their triangles to God's Spirit. At best, people on the first level follow a rational life and use moral guidance. These people are like anyone else in their world. They may be religious or nonreligious. They can be farmers or businesspeople or educators. They can be rich and famous, or they can be poor and insignificant. They are measured by the standards of their peers in the world. At worst, they are self-centered, exploiting others for profit and self-gratification.

People in the second level of living standards are in the world and aware of the presence of God. They are like natural trees expressing the desire to produce good fruit, but they avoid grafting. If they are grafted, they fail to cut off the natural limb that allows the grafted bud to grow. They use God according to their needs. Their spiritual commitments are short-lived and do not allow God to be their Lord. These people do not allow the Holy Spirit to function as the master disk of their lives. They intend to be good and God-loving people, but do not have the discipline to give full control to God. They are in the neutral zone, neither hot nor cold.

The third level of living standards is that of the grafted tree. These people allow God's Spirit to take charge of their inner beings. They are in the world but not of the world. They set their priorities as God's people, not like the people of the world. They know who they are and whose they are. They are not afraid to be different from the people of the other two levels. Their inner triangles are guided and controlled by the Spirit of God, and Jesus Christ is their Lord and Master. They allow the Holy Spirit to be their control file, filtering every thought and prompting every action. Jesus interceded to the Heavenly Father for this group of people:

> "I have given them your word, and the world has hated them because they do not belong to the world, just as I do not belong to the world. I am not asking you to take them out of the world, but I ask you to protect them from the evil one. They do not belong to the world, just as I do not belong to the world. Sanctify them in the truth; your word is truth. As you have sent me into the world, so I have sent them into the world. And for their sakes I sanctify myself, so that they also may be sanctified in truth" (John 17:14–19).

Living in the third level is to live in faith. It is climbing the hills, walking through the plains, and even moving through the valley of the shadow of death, exercising faith for the journey. Living life in this third level allows God to control all the triangles of our inner being. Here, we are consistently created and recreated in the image of God. Life in the third level allows us to live in the natural world and participate in the creative power of God. In this level, we place the Word of God within our inner beings, between the soul and the spirit, to discern the will of God. Here, we allow the creative energy of God to hover over every thought and bring newness of life in His way. We funnel all information of the mind through the Spirit of God and submit our entire intelligence and whole inner being to the creative Spirit of the Creator for new creation. This third level of life allows us to transcend beyond all rational possibilities of the natural realities and merge the human triangles with the triangle of God. We then experience the promise of Jesus and realize the oneness in the spirit with the Father, Son, and Holy Spirit. Living in the third level is living in the love of God. It is being online with God.

FAITH AND FEAR

Faith is the ability to transcend the inner being beyond the natural possibilities. Faith in God is exercising the inner being to interact with the Spirit of God. Faith in God allows us to plug into the creative energy of God for a new creation, bring all the members of the triangles in submission to the Spirit of God, and discover new possibilities with God. Faith brings every wish and visualization to God while being guided by the Spirit of God. It affirms that with God all things are possible, and it prays, "Not my will, but Yours be done" (Luke 22:42). Faith rises above our internal inhibitions and rational impossibilities.

Fear is a natural response of the rational mind. Reason seeks to control emotion from taking risks that might limit comfort or pleasure or lead to physical danger. Reason receives information from the mind and passes it to emotion. Reason associates the new information with the internal inhibitions to create fear, which in turn restricts a person from adventuring into new possibilities. Fear limits a person's potential and might intensify one's emotional pull. It can unbalance the basic working triangle and keep a person from rising above natural possibilities.

Faith in God helps us to conceive new possibilities. We are told that the sailors with Christopher Columbus were excited to accompany the great adventurer. After several days of storms on the treacherous sea, many of the sailors were frightened and sought to change Columbus's mind and turn back to the safety of their homeland. Many sailors and pioneers of new possibilities aborted the conceptions of faith because of their fear. Still, Columbus kept the faith and did not give in to the fears of his fellow sailors. The result of his perseverance was that he discovered a new continent.

FAITH AND RELIGION

Faith is not limited to people of religious beliefs. Faith, as a science of new creation, works for every human being. People who do not have a religious faith often exercise a so-called "gut feeling," an intuitive regenerative force that calls reason to submit to the hope of possibilities. Thomas Edison was not a religious person, but he exercised faith over fear and possibilities over impossibilities. He was persistent in his research and discovered many products that revolutionized the world. Practicing religious faith helps us not only to discover new possibilities but also to be in harmony with the Spirit of God. "Widespread among believers and unbelievers alike is the notion that faith means believing something to be true where the evidence is not sufficient to establish knowledge."[21]

The Bible gives examples of people who exercised their faith beyond sufficient knowledge. The most exemplary character is Abraham, who lived at a time unlike that of today. There were no governments to protect the people, no highways on which to travel, and no telephones, computers, fax machines, or internet through which to communicate. People lived in communities and looked after their own families, clans, and tribes. It was dangerous to enter another group's territory. In this time, Abraham heard God speak to him: "Go from your country and your kindred and your father's house to the land that I will show you" (Genesis 12:1).

Abraham believed in God and took the challenge. He risked his life, his family, and his possessions. He had to overcome the fear that cautioned him of the danger of such an adventure. He had to submit all the information in his mind to the God of his inner being and allow the Spirit of God to hover over his total being. Abraham demonstrated faith in God and obedience to His voice. Abraham had to exercise faith beyond his reason to allow God to bring him to new possibilities.

Faith is God's gift to us that enables us to fathom things beyond the possibilities of the natural world. Faith is not limited to reason, which is limited to the natural process of cause and effect. Reason is the safeguard that keeps a person submissive to the natural world. Faith is the transcendental ability of the inner being to move beyond natural limitations. It is the connecting link to the creative source to enter new possibilities of creation. The author of Hebrews describes faith as "the assurance of things hoped for, the conviction of things not seen. Indeed, by faith our ancestors received approval. By faith we understand that the worlds were prepared by the word of God, so that what is seen was made from things that are not visible" (Hebrews 11:1–3).

Faith is not contrary to reason. When reason forbids us to go beyond rational possibilities and prompts the emotional member of the basic triangle to stop taking the risk, faith reaches out to the God of all possibilities to go forward into the unknown. "Augustine and Aquinas think that there can be no conflict between faith and reason, though faith declares the truth of more than reason can prove; and that support which reason can give to faith in no way lessens the merit of believing."[22]

In the biblical account, the classic example of faith is Sarah and Abraham's anticipation of the fulfillment of God's promise of having a child. Sarah became old and lost her natural ability to conceive. Sarah and Abraham were called to exercise their faith in God's promise. The Creator God is not limited to natural processes. Nothing is impossible with God; therefore, all things are possible. Abraham and Sarah were called to believe in the limitless possibilities of God, who could have given them a child during their natural reproductive years; however, that required no faith. Therefore, the God of Abraham calls believers to exercise faith against impossibilities.

If we believe in the God of Abraham, then the Sermon on the Mount is not an impractical discourse of Jesus, but instead provides practical instructions for His followers. Jesus calls to His disciples to climb the mountain with Him. Jesus did not make His teaching easy for His followers; He asked them to work toward perfection.

Once, a rich man approached Jesus with good intentions and asked, "Good Teacher, what must I do to inherit eternal life?" The conclusion of Jesus's response was: "You lack one thing; go, sell what you own, and give the money to the poor, and you will have treasure in heaven; then come, follow me" (Mark 10:17, 21).

The young man went away sad because he had great wealth with which he did not want to part. The disciples were astonished and perhaps upset by such a hard response. They questioned Jesus, pointing out that it is almost impossible to enter the kingdom of God. Jesus responded that, with God, all things are possible (Mark 10:23).

THE LAW OF MOSES AND THE SERMON ON THE MOUNT

The descendants of Abraham were called Israel, or "children of God." On their journey from slavery to freedom, God led them through the wilderness for over forty years to teach them discipline. God revealed Himself to them as a "holy" God. God's holiness is highlighted throughout the Bible:

- "Who is like you, O Lord, among the gods? Who is like you, majestic in holiness, awesome in splendor, doing wonders?" (Exodus 15:11).

- "For I am the Lord who brought you up from the land of Egypt, to be your God; you shall be holy, for I am holy" (Leviticus 11:45).
- "Extol the Lord our God, and worship at his holy mountain; for the Lord our God is holy" (Psalm 99:9).

God instructed Moses to lead Israel from captivity to freedom. On their way to the land God promised to Abraham, God invited Moses to meet with Him on Mount Sinai. On Mount Sinai, Moses communed with God for forty days and forty nights. God spoke to him the covenant He would make with the descendants of Abraham, the children of Israel. This covenant was revealed in the laws, commandments, instructions, and guidelines for the Israelites to live as a holy people of God. God also gave Moses His instructions in written form on tablets of stone: "When God finished speaking with Moses on Mount Sinai, he gave him the two tablets of the covenant, tablets of stone, written with the finger of God" (Exodus 31:18).

These tablets of stone were the Ten Commandments, and keeping them showed obedience to God. When they were obedient to God, the Israelites were guided and controlled by God's Spirit. The people of Israel were called to be different: a separated and holy people. During their journey through the wilderness, the Israelites were called to practice the Ten Commandments as a way of life:

"Moses convened all Israel, and said to them: 'Hear, O Israel, the statutes and ordinances that I am addressing to you today; you shall learn them and observe them diligently. The Lord our God made a covenant with us at Horeb. Not with our ancestors did the Lord make this covenant, but with us, who are all of us here alive today. The Lord spoke with you face to face at the mountain, out of the fire . . . You must therefore be careful to do as the Lord your God has commanded you; you shall not turn to the right or to the left. You must follow exactly the path that the Lord your God has commanded you, so that you may live, and that it may go well with you, and that you may live long in the land that you are to possess'" (Deuteronomy 5:1–4, 32–33).

On their journey, the people did not fully obey God's commandments. Moses, greatly burdened in his heart, repeated God's instruction time and time again (read the book of Deuteronomy to understand the gravity of this teaching). After Moses died, his associate Joshua took command and continued teaching the law. At last, the Israelites entered the long-awaited Promised Land. Before Joshua died, he summoned the people of Israel and gave them his last instructions, with warnings of destruction for disobedience and promises of blessing for strict observance of the law. Throughout the history of Israel, the prophets instructed the Israelites to be faithful to God by obeying the law. Drought, famine, disasters, defeat in war, captivity by foreigners, and the destruction of their cherished temple were attributed to Israel's unfaithfulness to God through their disobeying the law. The prophets spoke on God's behalf and struggled with the Israelites. During their struggle, God revealed to them the upcoming redemption. The prophets announced the hope of God's Messiah, the one who would come to deliver all people from their sins:

> "For a child has been born for us, a son given to us; authority rests upon his shoulders; and he is named Wonderful Counselor, Mighty God, Everlasting Father, Prince of Peace. His authority shall grow continually, and there shall be endless peace for the throne of David and his kingdom. He will establish and uphold it with justice and

with righteousness from this time onward and forevermore. The zeal of the Lord of hosts will do this" (Isaiah 9:6–7).

Another prophet declared:

> "The days are surely coming, says the Lord, when I will make a new covenant with the house of Israel and the house of Judah. It will not be like the covenant that I made with their ancestors when I took them by the hand to bring them out of the land of Egypt—a covenant that they broke, though I was their husband, says the Lord. But this is the covenant that I will make with the house of Israel after those days, says the Lord: I will put my law within them, and I will write it on their hearts; and I will be their God, and they shall be my people" (Jeremiah 31:31–33).

Christians recognize Jesus of Nazareth as God's Messiah, the fulfillment of the prophecies. It is through Jesus Christ that a Christian enters a new covenant with God. Christians believe that Jesus is the Christ, the Son of the living God. They accept Him as their Lord and Master, their personal Savior. They are called to remember that Jesus did not come to abolish the law, but to fulfill it:

> "Do not think that I have come to abolish the law or the prophets; I have come not to abolish but to fulfill. For truly I tell you, until heaven and earth pass away, not one letter, not one stroke of a letter, will pass from the law until all is accomplished. Therefore, whoever breaks one of the least of these commandments, and teaches others to do the same, will be called least in the kingdom of heaven; but whoever does them and teaches them will be called great in the

kingdom of heaven. For I tell you, unless your righteousness exceeds that of the scribes and Pharisees, you will never enter the kingdom of heaven" (Matthew 5:17–20).

The Sermon on the Mount is the fulfillment of the law. It is not measured by human standards, but by God's. Therefore, in the eyes of the world, a person may not commit adultery with another person so long as the two are not physically involved. However, lust within the inner being is the working of the destructive spirit. It is prompted by the physical member of the outer triangle without guidance from God's Spirit, conceived by thought, nurtured by desire, and birthing sin. Sin unbalances our triangles. The Spirit of God and holy energy and the spirit of lust and destructive energy cannot dwell together. Emotion prompts lust, and lust pushes out the presence and power of God from the inner being. When lust wants to associate with the mind for action, we must give control to the Spirit of God to put our carnal nature to death. The Apostle Paul testified that he died daily for the sake of Christ. Such experiences are not judged by the world, but by the Spirit. In the eyes of God, murder is not only a physical act of killing a person but also an act born of emotion without the guidance of God's Spirit. Anger allows emotion to take control and unbalance the angles of the inner being. When we give control to God's Spirit to balance the angles, we can practice Jesus's teachings from the Sermon on the Mount.

Some Christians believe that salvation is the gift of God, and they receive it by accepting Jesus Christ as their Savior. Some of them advocate a "once saved, always saved" mentality and go on to live however they wish. Even if they join a church, but experience no change in their lives or lifestyles, these people continue to operate in the old nature. However, this is not Christianity. It is a religious practice worse than that of the legalistic Pharisees who tried to earn their righteousness by being obedient to the letter of the law, attempting to please God by tithing. Jesus pointed out that the Pharisees were hypocrites whose hearts were not right with God's Spirit.

Professing Christ as our Savior also includes the repentance of sin and changing of our lifestyles to coincide with how Jesus taught us to live. The religion of Jesus Christ is a call to commitment. It is the call to take up the cross and follow Jesus as disciplined followers.

The Apostle Paul, who highlighted the gift of God's grace for human salvation, did not stop practicing spiritual discipline. He said: "There is therefore now no condemnation for those who are in Christ Jesus . . . who walk not according to the flesh but according to the Spirit. For those who live according to the flesh set their minds on the things of the flesh, but those who live according to the Spirit set their minds on the things of the Spirit" (Romans 8:1, 4b–5).

To live according to the Spirit of God, Paul practiced spiritual discipline: "For through the law I died to the law, so that I might live to God. I have been crucified with Christ; and it is no longer I who live, but it is Christ who lives in me. And the life I now live in the flesh I live by faith in the Son of God, who loved me and gave himself for me" (Galatians 2:19–20).

The Sermon on the Mount contains the spiritual principles of holiness for which God called and separated people from both the Old Testament times and today, in the New Testament times. The following verses affirm this truth:

THE ANNOUNCEMENT OF
THE BIRTH OF JESUS AS THE SAVIOR

"Thus he has shown the mercy promised to our ancestors, and has remembered his holy covenant, the oath that he swore to our ancestor Abraham, to grant us that we, being rescued from the hands of our enemies, might serve him without fear, in holiness and righteousness before him all our days" (Luke 1:72–75).

CHALLENGE TO THE BELIEVER

"Since we have these promises, beloved, let us cleanse ourselves from every defilement of body and of spirit, making holiness perfect in the fear of God" (2 Corinthians 7:1).

"Clothe yourselves with the new self, created according to the likeness of God in true righteousness and holiness" (Ephesians 4:24).

"Pursue peace with everyone, and the holiness without which no one will see the Lord" (Hebrews 12:14).

"Therefore prepare your minds for action; discipline yourselves; set all your hope on the grace that Jesus Christ will bring you when he is revealed. Like obedient children, do not be conformed to the desires that you formerly had in ignorance. Instead, as he who called you is holy, be holy yourselves in all your conduct; for it is written, 'You shall be holy, for I am holy'" (1 Peter 1:13–17).

STUDY QUESTIONS

1. What are the three levels of life?

2. What is the relationship between faith and fear?

3. Why is Jesus important for our salvation?

4. What is the difference between the Law of Moses and the Sermon on the Mount?

5. How do you practice the Sermon on the Mount and live in the world?

CHAPTER
9

REMOVING INHIBITIONS
AND FRICTIONS

Webster's New World Dictionary defines inhibition as "anything that inhibits; esp., a mental or psychological process that restrains or suppresses an action, emotion, or thought." Inhibitions are innate and learned negative factors that work within the mind. They are fears, restrictions, taboos, and other contributing beliefs that limit a person's potential.

The mind is a complex storehouse of information. It operates on three levels: the conscious, the subconscious, and the unconscious. As we learned earlier, the conscious level has files of information that associate with new information for action. Conscious acts are originated and carried out by various members of the triangles. Therefore, every conscious act can be explained by the angles.

The most identifiable triangle is the basic working triangle made of reason, emotion, and morals. The subconscious level of the mind operates as the backup files of information. It is a silent partner, serving the conscious mind and occasionally taking control to protect the body from danger. When the conscious mind is resting, the subconscious mind takes over the responsibility of meeting the body's need. The subconscious is the great protector of the body, projecting the innate—and sometimes the inactive—information to the conscious mind for action.

The third level is the unconscious mind; think of it as the old files of information. The seemingly lost memories are not lost forever. They are stored in the inner chamber of the unconscious mind.

Fear is an emotion that warns the conscious mind of danger. If one is afraid of snakes, emotion warns reason to avoid snakes. To avoid snakes, one might stay away from the woods, desert, or other places where there might be snakes. However, the physical senses might make another part of emotion aware of the joys of the outdoors. To enjoy outdoor activities, you might use reason to inform emotion that not all snakes are poisonous and that snakebites are rare. When emotion does not have the courage of rational counsel, you might take measures out of fear, such as buying snake protection to calm emotion's concern. Thus, reason will meet emotion's need. In addition, reason will try to replace bad emotions with good emotions. One might hold courageous thoughts up against fearsome thoughts.

However, if—physically protected and mentally prepared—you come upon a snake, the immediate response comes from your subconscious mind, which works as a prime mover for quick action. Your subconscious might freeze the body, preventing movement before reason can respond for action. The subconscious mind has a built-in protection force, and it will react instantly to save the body from physical danger, like when you touch a hot surface and instantly pull back your hand.

The subconscious is a wonderful protector, companion, commander, and friend of the conscious mind. However, the subconscious is also an inhibitor. It is programmed by the collected strength of information and works as an accumulated and condensed information chamber for action and quick response according to the immediate need. Therefore, reprogramming the subconscious mind is important for removing negative inhibitions. It is not an easy task, but it is a possible one. It takes much discipline and practice to reprogram the subconscious mind to support the conscious mind without inhibition.

A Personal Experience of
Snakebite Fear as an Inhibition

I grew up in the southern tropical part of India where there are many poisonous snakes. In the fifth grade, I lost my close friend and neighbor to a snakebite from a venomous snake more poisonous than the cobra. The locals called it "the eight-foot killer" because, upon its strike, a person could walk only eight feet before falling and dying. I lived with a fear of snakes.

On a cool morning, I walked through a narrow trail covered in brush, overgrown from the recent monsoon rain. As I moved down the trail, I found a colorful rope lying across the path and bent to pick it up. My hand reached down, and the rope moved. I instantly froze. Even before my conscious mind could recognize that the rope was a snake, my subconscious mind informed my body to be still. Because I froze, the snake was either not aware of me or it did not perceive me as a threat. It did not strike me. When the snake slithered away, my rational senses told me to move away, too. I then saw it move to an open area, and my response was to throw a rock at it to kill it! I threw a rock and hit the snake on the head. It stopped running away.

As I analyze my past actions, I recognize that my subconscious mind took the action to freeze my body, keeping me from disturbing the snake. Throwing the rock was both a conscious and subconscious action. Upon disabling the snake, I came to my rational mind and called for help: a conscious act. A neighbor came and killed the venomous "eight-footer."

As a Christian, I attribute my deliverance from this snakebite and my response in that situation to God's protection. Using the triangle theory, this situation can be analyzed as God's Spirit controlling the triangles of my inner being, keeping all members of my triangles in harmony.

AN EXPERIENCE OF REMOVING THE FEAR OF SNAKEBITE AS AN INHIBITION

However, despite my protection in this situation, my fear of snakes did not go away. When I was older, I bought a parcel of land in East Texas because of my love for land and trees, but I was afraid to venture into the woods for over five years because of my fear of snakes.

One day, I went on my first hunting trip with a friend. I did not know anything about hunting with a rifle. My friend knew all about whitetail deer hunting and taught me how to use a rifle, giving me one of his rifles to use for the hunt. We went into the woods, and he asked me to wait on a spot from where I could see deer movements. I waited for game until it grew dark. I did not have a flashlight (this was before cellphones). My friend also did not have a flashlight. Neither of us knew which direction to walk. After some wandering through the woods, we listened for sounds, hoping to sense the direction of the road. I did not wear boots, as he had, but walking shoes. I was frightened by the possibility of being bitten by a snake, but I did not have any choice but to walk and find a way out of the woods. We walked through thick brush piles and dry creek beds, stepping down gullies and over the creek beds. We tried to listen for the sound of any motor vehicles to orient ourselves and find our way out of the woods.

After about forty-five minutes of walking through the unfamiliar woods, my friend—an army veteran—chuckled at my fear of snakes. I, however, was frightened about the possibility of a snakebite and prayed for God's help. I was glad when we finally heard the sound of motor vehicles and eventually found our way to the road.

When we got into our pickup and drove to a hotel, I realized that I had been freed from the fear of snakes forever. This experience was therapeutic for my conscious mind, allowing it to overwrite the inhibitions and fears I had stored in my conscious and subconscious mind for many years. Perhaps, in any future snake sightings, my subconscious will again freeze my body and keep me from danger. However, the fear of snakes as an inhibition no longer has the power over my conscious mind to stop me from enjoying outdoor recreation.

Walking without light and boots that day was my liberating experience to becoming a hunter. Over the last forty-plus years, I have never missed a deer hunting season. I have hunted in many rugged West Texas hills and plains—where rattlesnakes are known to hide in the holes of rock piles and creek beds—and I have hunted in many heavily-wooded areas of East Texas as well.

One way to think of the word *FEAR* is through this acronym: **F**alse **E**xpectation **A**ppearing **R**eal. A snakebite is a false expectation. Fear is a negative emotion that limits us from fulfilling the potential the Creator has invested in each one of us. When fear inhibits the conscious mind, we build up an invisible wall of protection. Fear as inhibition keeps us from flying on an airplane, befriending a stranger, attending a party, public speaking, feeling good about ourselves . . . the list goes on. Unchecked fear can paralyze us into depression.

In my years of pastoral counseling, I have encountered people who were afraid of flying for fear of the plane crashing. Even if they were to get a free plane ticket or receive a gift for a free trip abroad, they would find excuses not to use these gifts because of their fears.

I also counseled a person who witnessed the death of a teenager in a neighboring house; the house had caught fire with the teen still inside. Ever since that incident, this person was afraid to leave the house without someone else in the house. She worked for her husband but could not always go to work and was never on time. When she left the house, after traveling only a couple of blocks, she would turn around and come back to check that the stove was off. She would leave again, but before long she turned back to check the stove again. This paranoid repetition took a toll on her daily life.

Another form of inhibition appears as a compulsion. It often manifests as pleasure, lust, greed, and other kinds of destructive energy. For example, a friendship can be defiled by the inhibition of lust. A person inhibited by lust is compelled to look for opportunities to meet its demand. On one hand, fear as an inhibition keeps a person from facing the object of their fear. On the other hand, compulsion as an inhibition urges a person to reach for the object of pleasure. A fear-inhibited person thinks of danger and stays away from the object of danger. A lust-inhibited person thinks of pleasure and seeks the opportunity to possess it. In the working of the triangles, a member of a triangle who asserts or suppresses an action is the inhibitor.

THE WORKING PROCESS OF INHIBITION

Upon witnessing, reading, or hearing about a house fire, a person might begin to fear a house fire. This is the work of emotion, which keeps that information in the mind for protection from future fires. Reason counsels emotion to take precautions, such as keeping matchboxes and lighters away from children. However, emotion may further reject the counsel of reason and continue to accumulate more information about house fires. The fear of a house fire then becomes an inhibition in the individual, who—without balancing emotion with the help of reason and morals, the other members of the triangle—continues to keep fear of fire as an agent of control within the inner being.

When emotion is in control, it overtakes reason and morals and influences thought. When this happens, thought is not free from the fear of a house fire. Thought informs the mind—which in turn informs other members of the triangles—about the possibilities of fire. Reason continues to send information to the mind to remove every possibility of fire to satisfy emotion's demand. Emotion, now out of balance, produces destructive energy with even stronger fears of a house fire. Gradually, inhibitions impregnate thought, which then gives birth to paranoia. Paranoia becomes the cherished child of the individual. This child grows, making nagging cries and demands on the mind to ensure that all stoves are turned off before leaving the house or sleeping.

On the way to work, this child bursts out in a temper tantrum and demands thought to make sure that the stove is turned off. Under great distress, the individual returns home to make sure that all the knobs are turned off. This pattern repeats as paranoia grows, and the individual loses the ability to function normally. Such an individual will get up several times at night to make sure there is no fire anywhere in the house. This person may stop going to work to make sure the house will not catch fire, and they will not allow family members to partake in any outdoor cooking or other activities that involve fire. Such inhibitions can cause friction in relationships. Inhibitions destroy our human potential.

FRICTION

According to its definition, "friction" means a disagreement or conflict because of differences of opinion, temperament, and resistance to motion of two moving objects or surfaces that touch.

Internal frictions are disharmonies caused by the members of the triangles. External frictions are born out of relationships with others, the immediate world, and the universe. The stored information of the mind acts and reacts according to the incoming information and personal interest. For example, some people like blue, and some people do not. Some people like red, and others do not. People have many likes and dislikes, just as everyone is different. The intensity of people's likes and dislikes causes friction. Some likes and dislikes are innate personality traits. Others are learned likes and dislikes from the accumulation of information received from the immediate world. New information can create conflicts with the existing information in the mind. One person's behavior, words, attitude, value judgments, and other expressions can cause friction in the mind of another person. The possibilities of friction in human relationships are too many to list, but because of friction, people do not get along, marriages break down, friends become enemies, neighbors quarrel, and nations fight one against another.

WORKING PROCESS OF FRICTION

When a person hears, sees, reads, or experiences negative things about someone close to her, she might either respond quickly to resolve the matter, or she will store that information for future use. If the person is a family member, close friend, or neighbor, reason will counsel emotion to take quick action according to the emotional intensity of the situation.

Thought sends information to the conscious mind, which then sends it to the basic working triangles for evaluation and response. An unresolved negative thought about someone alerts the mind about any possible negative implications. Accumulated negative thoughts will become negative power points in the bank of information, producing negative action. These power points may cause hints of displeasure toward this other person, revealing these displeasures through words, attitudes, and actions. Soon, the other person also begins to keep negative information and create power points toward her. These two individuals might be close—family members, friends, or fellow church members—but the two live with negative feelings toward each other, eventually growing uncomfortable with and avoiding each other. In this state, both people harbor internal friction. When they face another negative situation, it might end up in external conflict. Such conflicts can, at best, cause unhealthy relationships and, at worst, destroy relationships.

We must remove any internal frictions to have harmony in our inner beings. Internal harmony—the state in which all members of the triangles work together—is important for external harmony. Internal harmony is the state in which no member of any triangle makes any demand upon the other members for action. This state appears to be the most inactive, but it can lead to creativity and greater possibilities, with all members working together to achieve a goal or goals.

To achieve this state of harmony, some people get away from society to find a place of quietness. Some choose a monastic lifestyle. The extreme form of such practice is seen in certain devotees of Hinduism. To achieve perfect inner harmony, these individuals depart from the daily duties and responsibilities of life and retreat to the mountains for meditation. This practice occurs at the last stage of their lives, between retirement and death. It appears to be a good way to end one's life on earth. However, it is an inactive state of life. For example, the body's natural survival needs make demands upon the members of the triangles, calling for action. Removing these needs from the members of the inner being is death. Healthy friction is vital for creativity and growth. We need this friction for the growth of our physical bodies as well as our minds. Our goal should not be to suppress or remove all interactions of the members; we should strive to guide them to work together in harmony. Paul explains his inner friction that drove him to grow in his faith:

> "For we know that the law is spiritual; but I am of the flesh, sold into slavery under sin. *I do not understand my own actions. For I do not do what I want, but I do the very thing I hate.* Now if I do what I do not want, I agree that the law is good. But in fact it is no longer I that do it, *but sin that dwells within me.* For I know that nothing good dwells within me, that is, in my flesh. I can will what is right, but I cannot do it. *For I do not do the good I want, but the evil I do not want is what I do. Now if I do what I do not want, it is no longer I that do it, but sin that dwells within me.* So I find it to be a law that *when I want to do what is good, evil lies close at hand.* For I delight in the law of God in my inmost self, but I see in my members another law at war with the law of my mind, *making me captive to the law of sin that dwells in my members.* Wretched man that I am! Who will rescue me from this body of death? *Thanks be to God through Jesus Christ our Lord!*" (Romans 7:14–25, emphasis mine).

The body of flesh and blood, bones and marrow is made of natural substances; it cannot survive without natural sustenance. Disconnecting it from the natural world leads to death and decay of the body. It cannot exist without nature's support, even for a small amount of time. Its basic survival needs are air, water, and food—basic elements necessary for the physical body, a member of the first triangle.

However, meeting the needs of only one member of the triangle family will not keep the body functioning. The body seeks security, leisure, pleasure, and reproduction. It cannot meet these needs without the help of the other members of the triangle family. Likewise, the other members cannot survive without the body. Meeting these needs alone makes humans mere creatures of nature. Indeed, meeting only these needs will not fulfill us because we are more than mere creatures of nature.

The body uses five senses to receive information from nature. The information is passed to the mind for action. Each member has its bank of information and associates that bank with the incoming information for action. When a member associates with incoming information and seeks to control the mind, it becomes an inhibitor. When a member forces its way, ignoring other members of the triangles or joining forces with another member for action, it causes friction.

The fear of suffocation—as an inhibition—might cause a person to live with claustrophobia, thus preventing him from riding in an elevator. It might cause friction in a relationship when he is one day forced to ride in an elevator. On a larger scale, the need for water and the fear of not having enough of it might prevent a person from sharing his water with his neighbors. This often happens in rural villages when the owner of a well prohibits a neighbor from drawing water. Such conflicts often end in quarrels. The fear of gaining weight—as an inhibition—might cause a person to stop eating, leading to anorexia. On the other hand, desire for more food can cause not only weight gain but also friction with those who do not have enough to eat. We see such behaviors among people in both poor countries and rich nations.

Inhibitions and frictions are not caused by material substance but by the members of the triangles. Within the material body we find the nonmaterial inner being. It is not made of flesh and blood but of eleven interconnected interactive triangle members connected with the twelfth member: the body. The working of these members and their relationship to other members of the inner being make every human uniquely different— happy or sad, good or bad, right or wrong, children of God or children of the devil. Understanding the working dynamics of these members is the key to achieving the desired goal of interaction.

The natural body sends information to thought for possible action. Thought is the connecting member of the body and mind. It is the conceiver of ideas, the source of motion in the inner being prompting the members of the triangles for action. Thought is in constant motion like the wind—sometimes strong like a hurricane, other times calm as a gentle breeze—and is always moving. Interaction, conception, and birth do not take place within a human being without motion. Without motion, the body is a wasteland, a hopeless field, a vegetative helpless state.

As the conceiver of ideas, thought passes information to the conscious mind for a response. The conscious mind passes information to other members of the triangles for their counsel for action. Other members of the triangles either accept or reject this new information. They might associate and join for action or disassociate and warn about the dangers of action. When any member of the triangles asserts the power to control the mind, inhibition or friction takes place. Removing these possessions that cause inhibitions and frictions within a member of one of the triangles is not an easy task. Those possessions are like that member's personal wealth. However, when one member of someone's triangles controls other members, that person suffers from mental illness.

ILLUSTRATION OF FRICTION

The following is a true story with fictitious names:

Robert and Renee are members of a small church. They are new to this church. John and Betty are longtime members of this congregation, and they walk and talk like they own the church.

Robert is the new chairman of the board. The board members are all in good spirits toward one another, seeking to build up the church by inviting prospects and welcoming the new members.

Betty allows a wedding in the church without consulting with the chairman and getting the board's approval. Robert does not like this. Several weeks later, Betty calls for a community meeting in the church without asking the board's permission. Robert protests, and Betty decides not to help Renee with Vacation Bible School (VBS). Renee is so upset with Betty that they do not talk to each other for weeks. Robert overhears Betty say to another member, "Well, I guess nobody cares about VBS." Robert and Renee see this jab as a retaliation. Robert resigns from the board, and the couple leaves the church.

The above example is a small friction compared to the common major fights in many church communities.

Leo Tolstoy, the great Russian novelist, wrote a story about two neighbors named Ivan and Gavrilo. Ivan's wife heard her hen cackling in Gavrilo's barn. She presumed that her hen had laid an egg in Gavrilo's barn and went to look for it. She could not find the egg. When Ivan came home, his wife told him about the incident. Ivan went over to Gavrilo's barn, and the two exchanged unpleasant words. Tearing their shirts in anger, they then fought physically. Later, at a wedding, Gavrilo struck Ivan's wife with his fist. She had to be hospitalized for a week. The judge ordered a punishment of fifteen lashes to Gavrilo. As Gavrilo was beaten, he murmured that he would take revenge by burning down Ivan's barn. Ivan saw Gavrilo set the fire and ran after him to catch him in the act, but Ivan failed to put out the fire. It burned not only his barn, but spread to his house, to his neighbor's house, and eventually to the entire village.

The above illustrations mention the friction caused by ancient hatred of ethnicities, color, national origin, and religious differences that have stirred up quarrels and wars. We see it throughout history, including Hitler's Nazi Germany and the extinction of six million Jews, the conflicts between Hindus and Moslems, and the ethnic cleansing in Rwanda, Bosnia, and Kosovo. This friction has manifested in protests against police brutality toward Black people in the United States.

THE GOD POWER REMOVES INHIBITIONS

The God power, the creative energy, is a greater power than all the destructive information accumulated in the triangles within the inner being. Faith in God is the key to overcoming destructive inhibitions and frictions that limit us. Faith in God is to submit our entire inner beings to God's Spirit. When inhibitions seek to impregnate your thoughts with fears of the impossible, invoke the Spirit of God to open new possibilities and empower you for new action. God's Spirit can guide and control all the members of your triangles. When inhibitions make your conscious mind aware of danger, invoke the power of the creative energy within you, "for the one who is in you is greater than the one who is in the world" (1 John 4:4). The Apostle Paul asked, "If God is for us, who is against us?" (Romans 8:31). Let faith work with the conscious mind to overwrite fears caused by inhibitions. Let the love of God's Spirit give you power over the inhibitions of fear born out of hate and prejudice. Invoke God's Spirit of courage to empower the members of your triangles to act courageously and overcome any inhibitions that limit your potential. Invoke the Spirit of God within your conscious mind to make sound judgments to avoid dangers. Sound judgment brings out all the available information from every member and allows the Spirit of God to guide them. Affirm to your subconscious mind that "with God all things are possible" (Matthew 19:26, NIV). Believe this and practice it so that your subconscious mind will listen to the voices of faith over the voices of inhibitions and doubts.

SELF-HELP TO REMOVE INHIBITION

First, you must believe. This changes your thinking and seeks to remove any inhibitions of doubt that limit you. Second, visualize good outcomes and give thanks to God for them. By practicing this exercise, you allow the creative energy of God to recreate your internal world. Repeat this process until it is engrained within your mind. Remember what the great Master Teacher taught: "Truly I tell you, if you have faith and do not doubt, not only will you do what has been done to the fig tree, but even if you say to this mountain, 'Be lifted up and thrown into the sea,' it will be done. Whatever you ask for in prayer with faith, you will receive" (Matthew 21:21–23).

For example, when you wake up with thoughts of impossibilities, repeat this phrase: "All things are possible with God." When you are about to face a task—and you made every preparation for it—such as going in for an interview, giving a public speech, or taking a test, and you feel like you will fail, practice autosuggestion. Say to your mind, "I am going to have a great interview; it will be my choice to accept or reject the offer." Say to your rational mind, "I am going to remember the answers, and I will pass this test," and impress this onto your subconscious mind: "My speech will be greatly admired by the audience." Visualize the audience applauding with great enthusiasm and give thanks to God for allowing you to speak. First, you believe and create a spiritual world; second, you create a new internal world; and third, you use spoken words—the building blocks of your new external world—to create a new reality.

BUILDING UP HARMONY TO REMOVE FRICTION

To build up harmony means to focus on the likable, positive, and agreeable attributes of another person. Often, thought sends messages to the conscious mind, and accumulated information in the subconscious mind associates those thoughts for action. If a person is unhappy with a relationship, the mind highlights the differences between them and the other person for action. Depending on the negative personality trait, this person might take immediate action or defer it to another time. The deferred differences, dislikes, and disagreements one keeps in their mind might stay dormant. Other members of the triangles will add this negative information to any incoming information. When negative information becomes stronger, emotion cuts off positive relationships, resulting in friction.

In relationships such as marriage, reason may work with its siblings to change one spouse to fit into the other spouse's desired mold. This results in one person manipulating the other through criticism and confrontation. Tension and unhappiness grow in the relationship, leading to marital strain and often ending in divorce.

Train your thoughts to focus on the positive things, like all likable and agreeable qualities about the other person. Think about the other's interests and find similar interests. Now, visualize both you and your spouse building upon those common interests and feel your differences lessening. Train thought to ruminate on the positive things about the other person rather than focusing on the negative.

The Apostle Paul wrote to the church in Philippi, "Do nothing from selfish ambition or conceit, but in humility regard others as better than yourselves. Let each of you look not to your own interests, but to the interests of others" (Philippians 2:3–4).

Make your conscious mind submissive to the Spirit of God through prayer. Channel your negative and disagreeable thoughts to the Spirit of God and ask Him to remove them from your conscious mind. Highlight within your conscious mind the areas of positive, agreeable, and likable things about the other person. Practice this regularly until these things are ingrained in your subconscious mind. Repeat this exercise to ensure that your subconscious mind does not highlight the differences and the dislikes, but the similarities and the likes. When two people practice this spiritual principle, their relationship becomes stronger and richer. The creative power of the Spirit of God can recreate our inner beings and help us grow stronger in our relationships through common interests, while the areas of disagreement melt away. The result of such an exercise not only removes friction but also builds up a positive relationship.

JESUS'S TEACHING ON RESOLVING CONFLICTS

Dealing with conflicts in relationships can vary according to one's investment in the relationship. We find in the following scripture Jesus's teaching about dealing with conflicts in the community of faith and friendship:

> "If another member of the church sins against you, go and point out the fault when the two of you are alone. If the member listens

to you, you have regained that one. But if you are not listened to, take one or two others along with you, so that every word may be confirmed by the evidence of two or three witnesses. If the member refuses to listen to them, tell it to the church; and if the offender refuses to listen even to the church, let such a one be to you as a Gentile and a tax collector" (Matthew 18:15–17).

First, resolving conflict is our responsibility. When we face conflict with another person, we should seek to resolve it as soon as possible. Conflict has the potential to implant our thoughts with negative information about the other person. Such an evil seed, if not uprooted, will grow fast and offshoot into misunderstanding and a broken relationship.

Second, when conflict is not resolved by a sincere one-on-one discussion, we are prone to think that we are right, and the other person is wrong. One or two impartial people of the same community should hear the complaint and give counsel to both individuals. If we do not want to listen and resolve conflict, we cause pain not only to the individual with whom we are in conflict but also to the entire community.

Third, a church community has the responsibility to hear the complaint, pray for the individuals, and give counsel to resolve the conflict. When a person refuses to abide by the counsel of a community of faith, he or she has no part in that community. However, when two people work together with a common interest in mind and focus on their strengths rather than their weaknesses, they can generate new energy and a healthy community.

STUDY QUESTIONS

1. Identify the difference between inhibition and friction.

2. In what way(s) do you experience inhibitions and frictions?

3. How would you remove inhibitions and frictions?

4. Are you willing to practice self-help suggestions and positive imaging to accomplish the desired outcome? Why or why not?

5. How can you practice the teachings of Jesus to remove conflicts?

CHAPTER

10

FULFILLING YOUR PURPOSE AND ENJOYING THE FULLNESS OF LIFE

Each of us should know our purpose in life. Jesus is our example. He had a clear understanding of His purpose. Faith in God is the vehicle that enables us to travel on God's highway towards fulfilling our purpose in life.

Jesus faced many obstacles on the path to fulfilling His purpose, including criticism, rejection, persecution, and even death. However, none of those things could change Jesus's mind against following the purpose God set before Him. He trusted God even with the possibility of the death of His physical body.

The Bible gives many examples of people who exercised their faith for the journey and fulfilled their purpose in life. When they submitted their purpose to God, their destiny became clear. As they traveled on God's highway, they carried on their purpose in life. Often, they were not able to see their purpose being fulfilled, and in those moments of doubts and fear, they had to exercise faith in God to travel on the long road to that fulfillment.

Following are some thoughts regarding finding and fulfilling your purpose:

1. Have a clear understanding of your purpose in life. Write it down.
2. Examine your purpose in the light of the Spirit of God and remove the possibilities of self-gratification and self-glorification.
3. Develop a step-by-step plan of action to fulfill your purpose.

4. Do everything you can to fulfill your purpose as though your life depends on it. Pray as though the entire matter depends on God.

5. Believe and visualize God enabling you to fulfill your purpose.

POSITIVE THINKING AND POSITIVE IMAGING

The late Dr. Norman Vincent Peale is acclaimed as the father of positive thinking. He wrote the book *Positive Imaging*, which explains how to take positive thinking to the next level through positive visualization. He gives many examples of people who have practiced this and succeeded with their dreams. The Bible gives many examples of positive thinking and positive visualization.

A good biblical example of positive thinking is Abraham, who is known as the father of faith. Joseph, Abraham's great-grandson, acts as another biblical example. He taught the principle of positive thinking and positive imaging; he was known as a dreamer.

> "He said to them, 'Listen to this dream that I dreamed. There we were, binding sheaves in the field. Suddenly my sheaf rose and stood upright; then your sheaves gathered around it, and bowed down to my sheaf.' His brothers said to him, 'Are you indeed to reign over us? Are you indeed to have dominion over us?' So they hated him even more because of his dreams and his words" (Genesis 37:6–8).

Joseph's brothers plotted to kill him, saying, "Then we'll see what comes of his dreams" (Genesis 37:20, NIV). Instead of killing Joseph, they sold him as a slave to some traders who were on their way to Egypt. The traders then sold Joseph as a slave to an Egyptian, one of Pharaoh's officials, the captain of the guard. The Bible tells us that God was with Joseph and he prospered. Joseph's master put him in charge of his household. God prospered the master's household because of Joseph. The master's wife lusted after Joseph and begged him to go to bed with her, but he refused, which got Joseph into trouble:

> "But he refused and said to his master's wife, 'Look, with me here, my master has no concern about anything in the house, and he has put everything that he has in my hand. He is not greater in this house than I am, nor has he kept back anything from me except yourself, because you are his wife. How then could I do this great wickedness, and sin against God?'" (Genesis 39:8–9).

Joseph revered God, but his integrity did not help him in this situation. The master's wife went after Joseph and tried to force him to have sex with her. He ran from her grip and left his outer garments, which she had grabbed. Out of anger, she made up a story and told her husband that Joseph had assaulted her. His master became incredibly angry and threw Joseph in jail.

Joseph stayed in the dungeon, with criminals, for two full years. He did not denounce God because of the evil he suffered, and he did not wallow in self-pity because of his innocence. He continued to believe in God. The writer of the book tells us that *God was with Joseph*. This is the key. Regardless of our situations in life, we must trust God and fully obey His will. After two years, Joseph was called to Pharaoh's palace to interpret Pharaoh's dream. Upon interpreting the dream, Pharaoh made Joseph the chief official of the palace, placing him in charge of the domestic affairs of the land.

"The proposal pleased Pharaoh and all his servants. Pharaoh said to his servants, 'Can we find anyone else like this—one in whom is the spirit of God?' So Pharaoh said to Joseph, 'Since God has shown you all this, there is no one so discerning and wise as you. You shall be over my house, and all my people shall order themselves as you command; only with regard to the throne will I be greater than you.' And Pharaoh said to Joseph, 'See, I have set you over all the land of Egypt.' Removing his signet ring from his hand, Pharaoh put it on Joseph's hand; he arrayed him in garments of fine linen, and put a gold chain around his neck. He had him ride in the chariot of his second-in-command; and they cried out in front of him, 'Bow the knee!' Thus he set him over all the land of Egypt. Moreover Pharaoh said to Joseph, 'I am Pharaoh, and without your consent no one shall lift up hand or foot in all the land of Egypt'" (Genesis 41:37–44).

Seven years later, when the lands around Egypt underwent severe famine, Joseph's brothers went down to Egypt to buy grain. According to Joseph's instructions, the steward took them to Joseph's house. Later that day, when Joseph came to his house, his brothers bowed down to him, as they had in Joseph's dream from many years prior. "When Joseph came home, they brought him the present that they had carried into the house, and bowed to the ground before him" (Genesis 43:26).

Upon the death and burial of Joseph's father, his brothers were afraid of retaliation, and they bowed down to Joseph, asking forgiveness: "Then his brothers also wept, fell down before him, and said, 'We are here as your slaves'" (Genesis 50:18).

Amazing, isn't it? With God, all things are possible. We must believe this and not allow the negatives and the fear of impossibilities to limit or destroy the potential God has invested within each of us.

Jacqueline Cochran grew up as a poor, orphan girl in a sawmill camp in Florida. She had only one year of schooling before she started to work at the age of eight. Jacqueline worked fourteen-hour shifts at a cotton mill in Georgia, for nine cents an hour. She mattered little in the eyes of the world. Whenever she saw an airplane, her heart soared with joy, and she wished she could fly to the stars. How could a poor woman with one year of schooling become a pilot? However, Jacqueline became the first woman to fly a supersonic jet and break the sound barrier. She said that the secret to her success was believing God's Word. As a child, she had heard a priest quoting this scripture: "Ask, and it will be given you; search, and you will find; knock, and the door will be opened for you" (Matthew 7:7). Jacqueline believed what she had heard about the promise of God and visualized flying beyond the stars.

Jessie Owens was born to poor Black parents in the Deep South, and later grew up in the ghettoes of Cleveland, Ohio. He was chosen to compete in the 1936 Olympic Games in Berlin. Adolf Hitler was determined to prove the superpower of the Aryan race. When Jessie walked into the arena, Hitler walked out. Fear took over Jessie in the presence of the hostile crowd and Hitler's champion, Luz Long. Twice, Jessie failed the qualifying jump. He was frightened and wished to kneel and pray, but without kneeling, he prayed and practiced faith in his heart, which he had learned from his parents as a child. Then, he felt a pat on his back. It was not the expected assurance of Jessie's coach, but rather Luz Long, his archrival. Long said, "Jessie, you can do it." Fear left Jessie's heart, and faith took over. He envisioned himself jumping beyond the qualifying mark and then broke the Olympic record. When the games were over, Jessie walked away with six gold medals as the super champion.

PLUGGING INTO THE POWER OF GOD

In preparation for this marvelous exercise, please read Psalm 139. Pay attention to verses 5 and 6. Understand that verses 19–22 do not refer to the enemies elsewhere, but to the enemies within us, destined to mislead us from our purpose of following the will of God.

God is Spirit. God is invisible energy and power. God is everywhere. Plugging into the power of God is connecting with God, which is experiencing the invisible reality of God in our inner beings. Plugging into God is communing with Him. He is greater than human knowledge, human reason, and all emotions. Plugging into God is greater than being a moral person, for He is greater than morals. Plugging into God is to bring all human triangles—reason, emotion, morals; body, soul, spirit; thought, desire, will; and conscious mind, subconscious mind, unconscious mind—into submission to God. It is allowing the greater power of agape love to indwell our inner beings, which then experience inner harmony.

God is love, and Jesus Christ is our example to follow the path of love. God's reality, His power, is available to everyone. First, Jesus submitted His life to God. Second, He went into the wilderness and sought God's mission and purpose for His life. Third, Jesus came out of the wilderness and manifested God's love in action as His purpose in life.

1. With the Word of God, Jesus identified His mission as God's mission.
2. He pointed out the unloving and unaccepting prejudices of religious people.
3. He accepted the people who were rejected by His own people.
4. He did not fight with those who rejected Him but went to receptive people.

5. He befriended people and invited them to join with Him to reach others.

6. He preached God's good news of love to all people.

7. He asked His followers to forgive their enemies and love everyone.

8. He embraced people who were poor and hurting and gave them hope.

9. He was willing to give away His physical body to reveal God's love.

10. On the cross, He prayed for forgiveness for those who were killing Him.

11. He gave away His body and entrusted His soul to God.

12. He rose from the dead as a living reality of God.

Plugging into this source of power is more than just believing in God. It is:

- communing with God and drawing from God's energy in every situation of life;

- energizing ourselves with the power of God's love and participating with the Spirit of the eternal God;

- not a casual matter or a simple religious belief;

- experiencing great power within our inner beings;

- the power that transforms us into the likeness of the divine;

- the power that changes a hateful heart into a loving heart;

- the power that replaces fear with courage;

- the power that allows us to forgive our enemies;

- the power that enables us to walk another mile even after walking a long road;

- the unending source of energy that works in every situation of life;

- the power that helps our inner beings to transcend beyond the natural limitations of the body; and
- the eternal Spirit that leads God's children to the presence of the eternal God.

FIRST: BELIEVE THAT GOD IS REAL

Believing is total submission to a reality that is beyond what the physical senses can experience. Reason needs physical evidence. Believing is submitting reason and all other associated members of the inner being to a higher power. Belief is not superstition, which is fear-oriented and rooted in cause and effect without basis. Contrastingly, believing in God is like love. When we believe, we experience inner change and connection with His positive and empowering Spirit. Believing is like the oxygen that sustains the physical body which, in turn, gives life to the inner being.

Believe that God is big enough to create the universe, yet small enough to interact with your inner being. Believe that God wants you to have the best in life and that you have the freedom of choice. You can choose right or wrong, good or bad. The Creator has given you this freedom. Believe that you are responsible for your actions and that the conception of every action takes place within your inner being. It is thought, one of the members of your inner triangle, that conceives an idea that then gives birth to an action. Commit your mind to conceiving not a single thought without the interaction of God's love. Train your thought to think through the Spirit of the Creator.

Second: Love God with Your Whole Being

God is love. Without loving God, you cannot plug into the source of God's power. Give thanks to God for loving you. Think about people who love you and the people whom you love. How do you experience their love? See that you relate to these people beyond physical relationships, beyond father, mother, husband, and wife. Within your inner being, experience the power of their love. If you are a child, give thanks to God for your parents who love you. If you are a parent, give thanks to God for your child.

Spend time in silence, away from distractions. Invite God's Spirit to come into your inner being and fill you with love. Look at God's creation and give thanks. Think on God's goodness toward you and give thanks. Say, "Come, Holy Spirit. Come into my heart and fill me with Your love." Sing songs of God's love in your heart and fill your inner being with gratitude. Let every member of your triangles experience the power of love. Start with your body.

Love Your Body and All Your Inner Being

Affirm this to your body: "You are lovable. You are God's gift. You are precious, lovely, and beautiful. You want to be healthy and strong. God loves you and wants you to be healthy and strong." Look at your hands and know that they are God's gift. God gave you your fingers. Love your hands and give thanks to God for them. Look at your legs, down to your feet, and know that the toes are God's gift. Affirm each part of the body and express love toward it. Give thanks to the Creator for making you the way you are. Invoke His creative energy to pass through every part of your body. Visualize the creative energy of God passing through your bloodstream.

Envision the power of God's love energizing your flesh and blood, bones and marrow. Commit to taking care of your body: eat what is good for you, get needed rest, exercise, and practice relaxation to make every part of the body work in the best way possible.

Tell your soul: "You are the life-giving member of my inner being. You make the members of the body work and the members of the inner being function. Without you I cannot exist on earth. You are indeed God's gift to me. Therefore, I give thanks to God for you."

Relax from all activities and rest for a while. Sit calmly, just giving thanks to God. Visualize the universe, God's magnificent creation. Sense God's Spirit of love filling your soul with love. Relax and give thanks to God again and again. Let your soul connect with the Spirit of God and experience the fullness of life, the love of God flowing into your soul.

Tell your spirit: "You are the activator of every action. I love you. Your attitude is the key to my actions. You can be humble or prideful, happy or sad, understanding or prejudiced, loving or hateful. You are the connecting link with the Spirit of God and the members of my inner being. You must keep yourself undefiled and clean so that the flow of God's energy will not be hindered. Let no member of the inner being mislead you. Let not the spirit of the destructive one corrupt you. Let the flow of the Spirit of God, His great love, be constant through you."

Take time to align your spirit with the Spirit of God. Examine whether any defilement or any hindrance blocks the flow of the Spirit of God. Seek oneness with the Creator in the Spirit.

Tell your reason: "You are a member of my basic working triangle. I love you. Without your work, I would be a fool and not act any better than the

beasts of the wild. You make me a useful person. You make me a rational being. I thank God for you. I pray that you will not be inhibited or influenced
by the forces of evil. Be impartial and always helpful to your immediate
siblings, emotion and morals. Let the love of God fill you with grace. Please
do not stay aloof in your own right; allow the creative Spirit to infuse you
with God's great love."

Tell your emotion: "You are God's gift to me. You make me feel good or
bad, loving or hateful, caring or angry. Without you, I cannot express love
and affection, joy or sorrow. I love you. I thank God for placing you within
me and making me the way I am. I pray that you will work together with
reason and morals. I pray that any other member of the triangles will not
lead you astray. Let the power of love fill you with strength and peace. Let
the assurance of the Creator be your strength in each moment of life."

Tell your morals: "You are special to me. You are God's gift within me to
keep me on the straight path and right road of life. You are my warning
signal when I go astray. You make me greater than all the creatures God
ever created. I love you dearly. I pray that you will work with your siblings,
reason and emotion, and you will not alienate one or the other. Be strong
and true when you are compelled to side with any members of the triangles."

Tell your thought: "You are the conceiver of ideas. I love you. Without
you, I would never grow. You are constantly moving my inner being with
new ideas and giving birth to new actions. I pray that the love of God
will be your faithful companion and that you will never commit adultery
against God's love. The charms of the evil one will not lure you away from
the true love of the Creator. Keep your gate closed for every message that
may mislead the mind to act with evil intent. Stand firm in the love of

God so that every member of the triangles will experience peace, harmony, health, and joy."

Tell your desire: "You are the motivator of my being. I love you. You move me forward to look for new opportunities and new possibilities. God has placed you within me so that I will participate in God's creation and enjoy life. I pray that you will not act without the consent of the members of the triangles. I pray that you will not act just to satisfy the natural needs of my body. Let the Spirit of Christ be your close friend, giving you counsel to follow a clean and wholesome path."

Tell your will: "You are the commander of every action. Without your permission, nothing will happen. You are precious to me. I love you. You have the power to act or not to act. You are given great responsibility. I pray that you will act in the interest of the Great Commander, your Creator, who placed you within my inner being. Please do not allow any member of the inner being to force you to act selfishly against God's love. Keep a cool head and follow the path of the Master, who showed you the way of life."

Tell your unconscious mind: "You have information of which I am not fully aware. You are my old files of information. I am glad that you are there for quick responses and especially in times of physical danger. I do not know how you operate. But, if you operate based on my past mistakes, I beg you to erase them forever. I pray that you will always remember the love of God in every action."

Tell your subconscious mind: "You are the companion, the silent partner of my conscious mind. I love you for being there. You give rest to my mind and take care of my being without any effort. You keep my body functioning as I sleep, and you act quickly to rescue me from danger. I thank God for you. You are my backup files of information. I pray that you will erase my sins and not act based on my mistakes. Allow the love of God to be there for me. When I act without God's love, please inform my conscious mind that I am in error. Remind my conscious mind to follow the path of love and peace, even during extreme situations that require a quick response."

Tell your conscious mind: "You are the essence of my whole being. You make me who I am. You are my active file, and without you, no action takes place. Your sharpness and punctuality are the keys to my success in life. Please do not limit your potential and become dull. Keep on adding new information and integrate it for action. I pray that the natural tendencies of the body will not control you. You can overcome the temptations of earthly desires. You will stand true and strong as a child of God, keeping the divinity the Creator placed within you to love God above all other members of the triangles. Let all your promptings be guided by God's love so that you will keep all members of the triangles in harmony."

Visualize that you are becoming "the salt of the earth and light of the world" (wherever you are, wherever you go, and wherever you will be is your world). Let the Spirit of Christ, the love that manifests as patience and kindness, radiate from within.

STUDY QUESTIONS

1. What is your purpose in life?

2. Can you relate to the example of Joseph in the Bible? In what way(s)?

3. What is the difference between positive thinking and positive imaging?

4. How can you practice spiritual discipline to subdue unhealthy habits?

5. Will you empower the members of your triangles and connect with God's Spirit to fulfill the purpose of your life? Why or why not?

CHAPTER

11

PRACTICE THE DISCIPLINE

Jesus showed us the example of taking time alone to bring His mind into full submission to God's Spirit. His experience in the wilderness was an intensely personal one, calling us toward a deeper commitment to follow God's will. After His experience in the wilderness, Jesus continued to practice spiritual discipline as a way of life. He often went away from the crowds and sometimes went away from His disciples to a private place to commune with God. Communing with God's Spirit brings all the members of all the angles in submission to the Spirit of God, energizing them with creative energy. Prayer and meditation are exercises that focus all the angles.

First, you must commit to follow a path of discipline. To make this commitment a turning point in your life, do something different from your routine to mark this new beginning. Fasting, writing a letter of commitment to God, giving up or adding something as a reminder of the path of discipline, or attending a spiritual discipline retreat can all serve as markers of this new journey.

Upon the marked beginning on your path of spiritual discipline, follow a daily routine of spiritual exercise. You might practice one or more of the following exercises while visualizing your triangles and following the love of God. Daily routines are important to overwrite old practices prompted by the old files. Daily routines train the subconscious mind with new information to act differently.

Your goal as a child of God is to be the "salt of the earth and light of the world." Keep this in your mind as a mantra, tune, or thought. When you fail to do this—which will happen—do not give up; instead, pray to God to fill you again and again with His Spirit, to add sweetness in your interactions with others as you manifest the grace of God as the light from within you.

ONE-MINUTE EXERCISE

1. WHEN YOU WAKE UP

When you wake up, affirm that the Spirit of God is in control and that you are going to walk with God all day long. Visualize yourself as a balanced triangle—the outer triangles submitting to the inner triangle—and view God's creative energy flowing from within and balancing your angles all day long. This is the Spirit of God controlling your inner being. Visualize the creative energy empowering you to practice integrity over dishonesty, courage over cowardice, faith over fear, love over hate. Believe that you are going to have a great day, that you are going to enjoy life, and that you are going to be a positive influence all day long. Affirm that you are creating your world, filled with the presence and love of God, around you. Remember that the definition of love is "patient and kind." Regardless of the situation, be patient and kind in your interactions with others.

2. WHEN YOU LIE DOWN TO SLEEP

When you lie down to sleep, give thanks to God in your heart for the positive energy you received during the day for your physical, mental, and emotional needs. Give thanks to God for the spiritual empowerment you received to practice love by being patient and kind. Ask God to forgive the mistakes and failures you made during the day and commit to improving. Pray for others as you close your eyes to sleep. Believe that God will grant you a restful night and that you will wake up refreshed in the presence of God. You might say, "I invoke rest: rest to my feet, rest to my mind, rest in God, rest through the night. Amen." Pray for people in your heart until you fall asleep. If you fail to sleep, think about people who have made a positive difference for you and pray for them. You might want to make a list of people you would like to pray for and continue this routine.

Follow this exercise format every day until it becomes a routine.

FIVE-MINUTE EXERCISE
(IN ADDITION TO THE ONE-MINUTE EXERCISE)

1. WHEN YOU WAKE UP

Read a devotional or a passage of Scripture. Ponder it with your conscious mind and place a positive thought from it in your mind—thoughts such as love, peace, joy, friendship, care, sacrifice, charity, courage, character, forgiveness, goodwill, etc. Pray and bring all your thoughts in submission to God's Spirit. Ask God to guide you all through the day, energizing your spirit with the thought of the day. Visualize yourself as a balanced triangle: the outer triangles submit to the inner triangle, and God's creative energy flows from within and balances your angles all day long. Visualize the creative energy empowering you to practice integrity over dishonesty, courage over intimidation, faith over fear, and love over hate. Believe that you are going to have a great day and that you are going to be a positive influence all day long. Pray for others. Lift them up to God in your mind and invoke God's presence upon them. *Keep this thought at the forefront of your mind: "Today, I will be salt of the earth and light of the world."*

2. BEFORE YOU LIE DOWN TO SLEEP

Read a devotional or a passage of Scripture and ponder it by placing its message within your triangles. Recollect the activities of the day and examine whether your angles were balanced or imbalanced. Pray for forgiveness of the mistakes you made and forgive others for their mistakes. Cleanse your thoughts and give thanks to God for the day's blessings. Give control to God's Spirit over your fears and anxieties. Pray for others and invoke God's protection and care upon them. Believe that God will grant you a good night of rest and a great day tomorrow.

TEN- TO THIRTY-MINUTE EXERCISE, ANYTIME

Read a passage of Scripture or a devotional and reflect upon it. See how it applies to your life. Examine your inner being to see whether any member of your triangles is alienating any other members. Is any member of the triangles taking the lead and creating power points for action? Do you have any angry thoughts, resentments, unholy desires, or anything else unbalancing your angles and diverting the flow of God's creative energy? Evaluate your total being: the members of the triangles. Are they all working together? Ask God's Spirit to take control. Change your thoughts toward any person who may have made you angry or resentful. Remember the teaching of Jesus in the Sermon on the Mount: "But I say to you, Love your enemies and pray for those who persecute you, so that you may be children of your Father in heaven" (Matthew 5:44–45). Seek to do something good to the individual who has upset you. Remember that any unforgiving thought will force your emotions to create power points, which will block the flow of the creative energy of the Spirit of God.

After cleansing your thoughts, visualize yourself as a balanced triangle: the outer triangles submit to the inner triangle, and God's creative energy flows from within and balances your life. Visualize the creative energy empowering you to practice integrity over dishonesty, courage over intimidation, faith over fear, and love over hate. In the morning, believe that you are going to have a great day and that you will be a positive influence all day long. In the evening, give thanks to God for a great day and believe God will grant you a restful night.

At other times of the day, gather your thoughts and follow the above suggestions. After examining your inner being and balancing your angles, pray for others. Intercession is a powerful spiritual exercise, invoking the creative energy of God upon others. Think about the people who need physical healing, emotional strength, spiritual empowerment, and who have other needs and concerns you might be unaware of. Lift those people in your heart to God and invoke God's creative energy for each one and each situation.

You might want to write in a journal a summary of the previous day and the expectations you have of the new day. You could list the anticipated activities of the day and add to it the needs and concerns of others. You might want to write a prayer, a poem, or a letter to God.

PRACTICE SPIRITUAL DISCIPLINE EVERY DAY

Establishing a routine of daily readings of positive thoughts, Scripture passages, or daily devotionals based on the Scriptures helps to balance the angles.

Our earthly bodies are the dwelling place of God's Spirit. In addition to practicing spiritual discipline, have the physical discipline of daily exercise as well as healthy eating to keep the body in shape.

CHAPTER

12

Forty Daily Devotionals

Practice these daily devotionals and experience change within your inner being.

DAY ONE

In the beginning when God created the heavens and the earth . . .
GENESIS 1:1

*In the beginning was the Word, and the Word
was with God, and the Word was God.*
JOHN 1:1

When did time begin? When will time end? What did God do before the creation of the heavens and the earth? Who created God? Our minds cannot fathom these concepts, much less answer these questions. Infinity is immeasurable. We are finite creatures, and we cannot grasp infinity with our finite minds. Before the technology of the internet, it was difficult for some people to comprehend the concept of God being omnipresent: everywhere at one time and available to everyone simultaneously. However, the internet proved that a message can be heard and responded to in many places at the same time.

God is Spirit. God is energy. God is the creative force. God is like a mighty mountain, immovable and strong. He is like a parent protecting and providing for His children. He is like a river, flowing with living water. God is like air, everywhere at once. Jesus Christ revealed the true nature of God as love. God is holy, undefiled, 100 percent pure love.

I was born, not by my choice, but as a gift of the creative power. I am in the universe, and I am part of the universe. The Creator has given me the power of choice. In the universe, I have the freedom to draw power from the creative force or ignore it. I also have the freedom to misuse the gifts God has invested in me. I must draw power from the creative force to overcome destructive forces and fulfill the purpose of my life. I choose Jesus Christ as my example to understand God, draw power from the creative energy, and enjoy life.

PRAYER:
God, you are the creative energy, sufficient for me.
I thank you for Jesus Christ, who showed the way.
Today, I choose to live in touch with you through Jesus, my Lord.
Help me brighten my world today through my words and deeds
With the power of love, like that of Jesus of Nazareth. Amen.

Believe that God is in you. God is the creative energy. God is love. Visualize the creative energy balancing the angles of your inner being.

Believe today that you will be salt of the earth and light of the world.

DAY TWO

The earth was a formless void and darkness covered the face of the deep,
while a wind from God swept over the face of the waters.
GENESIS 1:2

Have you had an opportunity to watch a potter working with a potter's wheel? The potter works with the clay through different stages. In the early stage, the potter is dirty and muddy. The clay is formless and shapeless. It is a blob. However, the potter does not leave it in that shape. He places it on the wheel and works with it, shaping it in the way he likes. Then, the potter burns the clay in the fire to cure it and make it strong.

When I asked a group of young people to describe the world before God's creation, they said that it was like a blob. Well, what made the difference? The creative energy of God hovered over the blob. The Spirit of God—the creative energy—brought forth order out of chaos, light over darkness, and life from inanimate substance. God shared with human beings His creative energy. We can create, shaping and reshaping the substance in the natural world. Look at a carpenter shaping wood, an architect designing, an engineer manufacturing, and a worker producing new products. God's creative energy is at work through humans in many ways.

When we allow the creative energy of God to hover over our inner beings, we become partners with God in shaping and reshaping our world. With God's creative energy at work, we can bring forth order out of chaos, creativity, and beauty. Our inner beings will experience peace and harmony. We will oversee and control our world, rather than have the world control us. We will build up our marriages, families, and other relationships. Our work, play, or whatever else we do will manifest the spirit of joy and thanksgiving.

PRAYER:
Lord, let your creative energy hover over my inner being
And bring order out of chaos, instilling creativity and beauty within me.
May your Spirit hover over my anxious thoughts, shaping me
And helping me to be a peacemaker in my troubled world. Amen.

Visualize God's power from the inner triangle sending creative energy to the outer triangles, calming anxious thoughts, removing fears and worries, and making you a creative and loving person.

Believe that you will be salt of the earth and light of the world.

DAY THREE

*Yet whatever gains I had, these I have come to regard as loss because
of Christ . . . I want to know Christ and the power of his resurrection
and the sharing of his sufferings by becoming like him in death, if
somehow I may attain the resurrection from the dead.*

PHILIPPIANS 3:7, 10–11

The outer shell of a seed must die to bring forth a new plant. An alcoholic must give up alcohol to be sober. Students must give up partying for the good of their studies. A mother must give up uninterrupted sleep for her newborn child. Life's success depends on the exchange value. Every day and every hour we exchange one thing for another. One can exchange idleness for action, hate for love, and comfort for adventure, or the opposite can take place.

The Apostle Paul testified that he set a goal and exchanged whatever he once considered profit for the sake of Christ. To achieve his goal, he made exchanges. He exchanged his reputation as a prominent Jewish leader to become a disciple of Jesus. As a result of this exchange, he suffered persecution. He exchanged wealth and fame for a life of following Jesus. As a result, he suffered hunger and pain. To a rational-minded onlooker, he made foolish exchanges, but Paul knew the purpose for his life.

With the purpose for his life in mind, Paul set a goal and made exchanges to achieve that goal. He said, "But this one thing I do: forgetting what lies behind and straining forward to what lies ahead, I press on toward the goal for the prize of the heavenly call of God in Christ Jesus" (Philippians 3:13–14). In his journey toward the goal, Paul had to make another exchange. He said, "I have been crucified with Christ; and it is no longer I who live, but it is Christ who lives in me" (Galatians 2:19–20). He declared the result of his exchanges: "I can do all things through him who strengthens me" (Philippians 4:13). It sounds like Paul achieved his goal. However, he did not stop. He continued on his path of spiritual discipline, and the result was great joy. Paul's letter from a Roman prison was filled with happiness. He wrote, "Rejoice in the Lord always; again I will say, Rejoice" (Philippians 4:4).

PRAYER:
Dear God, help me to make good exchanges with my time, money, thoughts, words, and actions. Help me to focus on my purpose and journey toward the goal. Grant me strength and courage each day. Amen.

Visualize your outer triangles giving control to the inner triangle of God's Spirit.

Believe today you will be salt of the earth and light of the world.

DAY FOUR

Even youths will faint and be weary, and the young will fall exhausted;
but those who wait for the Lord shall renew their strength,
they shall mount up with wings like eagles, they shall run
and not be weary, they shall walk and not faint.
ISAIAH 40:30–31

Life is a journey. Despite calculated planning and careful preparation, we will face unexpected obstacles along the way. We can prepare for flat tires, run-down batteries, and mechanical failures. Unfortunately, life's journey does not depend on the mechanical condition of our vehicles. Life's journey depends on our inner strength.

When you face the unexpected, how will you handle it? When the doctor's office calls and gives you the bad news, how will you deal with it? When your spouse shuts the door in your face, how will you react? When your children rebel against your values, how will you respond? These and the other endless questions of life can exhaust you. Where will you turn for creative energy? Do you have a dependable and inexhaustible source?

Several years ago, I was at a retreat center on a lake in Oklahoma. A siren sounded the warning of an approaching storm. Soon, the lake was clear of boats, and the golf course was emptied of players. Everyone hurried indoors. In its fury, the storm twisted up trees, stripping them of their leaves and limbs. I looked through the window, and in the far distance, above the vast, open lake, I saw an eagle flying above the storm!

During the storms of life, do not depend on your own energy that can corner you into silence. Instead, invoke the presence of God and believe that "the one who is in you is greater than the one who is in the world" (1 John 4:4). With God, you can fly high above the storms of life.

PRAYER:
Loving God, I believe in Your inexhaustible power.
Your power is sufficient for me to face the storms of this life.
Grant me the courage to submit my anxious mind to Your power
And to wait on You patiently for the flight over the storms of life. Amen.

When you face the storms of life, let not your outer triangles act without the power of the inner triangle. Visualize God's power flowing from within and calming anxious thoughts.

Believe today you will be salt of the earth and light of the world.

DAY FIVE

Do not fear, for I am with you, do not be afraid, for I am your God.
ISAIAH 41:10

Fear is a reality. Unhealthy fears inhibit the mind and hinder us from actualizing our potential. A person might not drive a car because of their fear of having an accident. One may not enjoy the outdoors because of their fear of snakes. Yet another will not fly because he fears plane crashes.

Fear may sometimes take control of a person's inner being in the form of worry, which robs a person's joy of life. Jesus taught His followers not to worry but to trust in God to overcome those fears that cause worry. The root cause of worry is the fear of losing oneself. Jesus said: "For those who want to save their life will lose it, and those who lose their life for my sake will find it" (Matthew 16:25). Jesus taught us how to overcome the fear of losing. He did not give in to the fear of what people thought about Him. Jesus did not give in to the fear of what people would do to Him. Rather, Jesus focused on the purpose of His life. His love for the heavenly Father was greater than His fear of losing. His focus on the heavenly Father's mission was stronger than the fear of danger. Therefore, Jesus did not give in to the fear of crucifixion. In the garden of Gethsemane, in uttermost anguish, He prayed: "My Father, if it is not possible for this cup to be taken away unless I drink it, may your will be done" (Matthew 26:42, NIV). Crucifixion was the worst form of losing oneself. Crucifixion meant losing one's dignity, self-worth, and life itself. Jesus's love for the heavenly Father was greater than His fear of crucifixion.

John, the beloved apostle of Jesus, learned this truth and wrote: "God is love, and those who abide in love abide in God, and God abides in them . . . There is no fear in love, but perfect love casts out fear" (1 John 4:16, 18). Love is the creative energy of God. When the outer triangles bring up unhealthy fears, you invoke the love of God.

PRAYER:
Loving God, please help me to focus on the purpose of my life.
Release me, Lord, from the captivity of fears that inhibit my mind.
Grant me the courage to trust You with all of my heart all of the time.
Fill me with Your love that I will not become a captive of fear. Amen.

Visualize the love of God becoming stronger in you and giving you the courage to focus on the purpose of your life.

Believe today you will be salt of the earth and light of the world.

DAY SIX

The earth is the Lord's and all that is in it, the world, and those who live in it.
PSALM 24:1

God is the creative force, and God created everything. He created a magnificent universe. Take a mental journey through God's creation. Look at the tall mountains with their snowcapped peaks, the valley below flowing with rivers, the tall pine trees, the mighty oaks, evergreen cedars, climbing vines, and flowering bushes. Notice deer and rabbits, mountain goats and squirrels, raccoons and possums, and countless other creatures in the wild. Look at the stream below. Clean and clear water rushes over the rocks. See the fish and other creatures in the stream. Sit at its bank under a shady tree. Enjoy the beauty, pure and serene. Walk through a trail in the woods, smell the wildflowers, and praise the Creator for this beautiful world.

Now, imagine you are standing on a sandy beach. Walk on it and feel your feet, seek a better grip. Reach down and take a handful of sand. Rub the sand between your hands and fingers and enjoy its fine texture. Look for a seashell and pick it up. Sit on the sand for a moment. Let the oncoming waves touch your feet. Watch out—the higher waves might get your clothes wet! Walk in the edges of the oncoming waves. Be careful: the sand could break away, and your feet could go deeper into the water. Watch the seagulls flying and the surfers gliding over the water. Rejoice in the Lord and give thanks.

Perhaps today you cannot physically go to the mountains or the beach, but you can take a walk in your backyard or a nearby park. Sit under a tree and enjoy some fresh air. Watch the clouds move and praise the Lord your Creator. Praise the Lord for the sunshine and the rain. Praise the Lord for the flowers and the trees. Praise the Lord for the birds and the squirrels. Praise the Lord for all His creation and for the gift of life.

PRAYER:
Loving God, I praise You for Your wonderful creation and
For Your gift of imagination that helps me travel far and wide.
Fill me, Lord, with love and gratitude that I will rejoice in You.
Help me, Lord, that I will be a blessing to someone today. Amen.

Think of the goodness of the Lord and meditate on the blessings of life.

Believe today you will be salt of the earth and light of the world.

DAY SEVEN

*So God blessed the seventh day and hallowed it, because on it
God rested from all the work that he had done in creation.*
GENESIS 2:3

Holy, Holy, Holy is the Lord of hosts; the whole earth is full of his glory.
ISAIAH 6:3

The Almighty God stopped everything on the seventh day! God gave us an example of rest. The seventh day is for stopping our routines, for rest and rejuvenation. Rest is vital for the human body. Of course, God could have kept creating. He did not and could not get tired. But God, like a loving parent, gave us an example of how to live. God created us out of the earth, and our earthly bodies need rest. A tired body has a negative influence on the mind. The Apostle Paul reminded us that our bodies are the temples of God. We must take time to rest from all labor to give room to God, the holy Creator.

Holiness is the state in which all members of our inner beings are in harmony, which allows us to be in harmony with God, the Creator. Holiness removes hindrances and allows God to dwell in us. Giving thanks to God is an important key to being at peace with God. Being with people who recognize God's love is important for empowerment. As a child of God, follow the teaching of God's Word. Every excuse a person makes against rest on the seventh day, choosing to not worship God, is an act of unbalancing the angles. On the Lord's Day, worship God with believers, repent of every act that caused your angles to become unbalanced. Examine your priorities in the light of Scripture and in consideration of your purpose in life. Use your spiritual gifts for the building up of God's kingdom. Meditate on God's Word. Consider praying the following prayer throughout the day.

PRAYER:
Fill me, Lord, with Your presence today.
Fill me, Lord, with Your power today.
Fill me, Lord, with Your love today.
Fill me, Lord, with Your joy today.

Make me a blessing today, dear Lord,
Make me a blessing to Your people.
Make me a blessing to Your world.
Make me a blessing throughout the week. Amen.

Think on the things of God and seek how you can be a blessing to someone.

Believe today you will be salt of the earth and light of the world.

DAY EIGHT

Then God said, "Let there be light" and there was light . . .
and God separated the light from the darkness.
GENESIS 1:3–4

At the beginning of creation, the universe was a blob, and it remained underwater in darkness. The creative power of God brought light out of the darkness and order out of chaos. The Spirit of God is power. It is creative energy. It is ours to use today to make the best of life.

Order or disorder: that is our choice. Sometimes, it might appear that we are not in control. Papers on the desk pile up, one on top of another. They then fall and get mixed up. Now we do not know where to even begin to sort the mess. Young children cry for attention while we must complete an important task. Interferences make it hard to concentrate. Problems arise, one after another, and we do not know where to turn or what to do. A telephone call brings bad or sad news. We are pressed too hard, and we do not have time to plan the day. Our health fails, and we have no control. Whatever the situation, please believe that you are not alone. If you give in to pressure, you are living in this blob state. You must rely on the creative energy to bring all members of your triangles to work together.

You can invoke the presence of God and draw energy from the inner triangle (Father, Son, and Holy Spirit) to the outer triangles and balance all the angles. Sing praises to God and meditate on God's Word. Let the creative energy of God's Spirit take charge of your life. Do not be afraid but be courageous to order your day. Make plans and stick to them. You have God's unlimited power available to you. Therefore, smile and do not frown. Use empowering words, not discouraging words. Pass on compliments, not complaints. Ponder new ideas, new directions, new possibilities, and new opportunities for life. Today, take charge of your thoughts and ask God to help you create a new world within you and around you.

PRAYER:
God, you are my strength today. Help me to calm my anxious thoughts, bring order out of disorder, and peace out of trouble. Please grant me Your creative power and lead me on the path of holiness. Dear Lord, please surround me with Your presence today, I pray. Amen.

Visualize the creative energy of God balancing all the triangles and bringing order out of disorder. Believe that, with God, all things are possible.

Believe today you will be salt of the earth and light of the world.

DAY NINE

*All things came into being through him, and without him not
one thing came into being. What has come into being in him was life,
and the life was the light of all people. The light shines in the
darkness, and the darkness did not overcome it.*

JOHN 1:3–5

Sometimes it is hard to comprehend the relationship between God and Jesus Christ. As Christians, we do not believe in three gods; so how then do we understand the concept of Father, Son, and Holy Spirit? We need to understand God as power, the creative energy. God is revealed in the personality of a loving Father, in the personality of a caring Son—who identified as a friend and Savior—and in the personality of a close companion, the Holy Spirit.

Jesus of Nazareth was born as a human child. He grew up like a normal child: He ate, slept, and carried out all other human activities. It is through this human being that the creative energy of God was revealed to people. The power manifested through Jesus is the same power that was at work at the beginning of God's creation. Just as God brought order out of chaos in the universe, Jesus brings order out of chaos in the lives of people. Just as God brought light out of darkness, Jesus brings God's light into our lives and removes spiritual darkness. Just as the sun and moon declare the glory of God's creation, the attitudes and actions of the followers of Jesus shine for the glory of God.

Jesus showed power through His example of loving those who hated Him. Jesus reached out to the rejected and downtrodden people. He brought them hope and led them to accomplish the purpose of their lives. Jesus of Nazareth, who lived long ago in Galilee, is still alive as one with the Father and the Holy Spirit to give power to God's children.

PRAYER:
Lord, fill me with Your power today, the power of your fatherly love.
Lord, fill me with Your power today, the power of your motherly love.
Lord, fill me with Your power today, the power of your Son, Jesus.
Lord, fill me with Your power today, the power of the Holy Spirit. Amen.

Visualize the loving presence of God as loving parents surrounding you, the caring presence of Jesus like a brother embracing you, and the guiding presence of the Holy Spirit leading you.

Believe today you will be salt of the earth and light of the world.

DAY TEN

There was a man sent from God, whose name was John. He came as a witness to testify to the light, so that all might believe through him.
JOHN 1:6–7

John the Baptist was born as a miracle child to his older parents. John had a purpose for his life. He called the Jewish people to repent for their stubborn and sinful hearts. He sought to prepare them to accept the arrival of God's light. John had a strong personality. He did not compromise God's message to please his listeners. He told God's truth to the Jewish religious leaders and to the ordinary folks alike. He confronted people's sins without fear. He was a truth-telling messenger. When people asked him about his purpose, he said that his purpose was to be a voice in the wilderness announcing the coming of God's light. He came as a forerunner to tell the people of the coming of Jesus Christ as the Light of God in the world.

The Jewish people respected John the Baptist and believed his testimony. He pointed them to Jesus and said, "Behold, the Lamb of God, who takes away the sin of the world!" (John 1:29, ESV). Even though people accepted John and his testimony, they were afraid to accept Jesus. Accepting John's testimony was like accepting a graft to become a new tree or installing a new control disk over the existing files in the computer. Accepting Jesus was a call for transformation to listen to the Spirit of God over the voice of tradition. Perhaps it was frightening to give up old ways of thinking for new ways of thinking, so many people rejected John's call for change.

We must be both willing to hear and courageous to follow God's truth at all costs. God's Word is the truth that liberates us from every fear. Jesus said, "If you continue in my word, you are truly my disciples; and you will know the truth, and the truth will make you free" (John 8:31–32).

PRAYER:
Loving God, thank You for John the Baptist.
I thank You for all your people who proclaim the truth.
Today, grant me the wisdom to hear Your words and follow Your truth,
And the courage to keep Your words in my heart and to tell the truth, I pray.
Amen.

Believe in the transforming power of God's Word as it liberates you from every fear and helps you to follow Jesus as a true disciple.

Believe today you will be salt of the earth and light of the world.

DAY ELEVEN

But to all who received him, who believed in his name, he gave
power to become children of God, who were born, not of blood
or of the will of the flesh or of the will of man, but of God.
JOHN 1:12–13

One day, a stray kitten came by our house. Our six-year-old boy brought the little creature inside. He played with this cat and fell in love with it. Our son did not want to let it go; he wanted to keep it as a pet. We searched the neighborhood to find its home, yet no one claimed ownership. So we adopted this little kitten as our pet. We gave it a name: Tiggi. We bought cat food and took it to the veterinarian and gave it the needed shots. It was no longer a stray cat but a beloved pet of the family.

God, through Jesus Christ, adopted us as members of His family. Becoming a child of God is to enter into a relationship with Him. It is being born again. When Jesus told this to Nicodemus, a teacher of the Jewish law, he was surprised and asked, "How can a man be born after having grown old? Can one enter a second time into the mother's womb and be born?"

Jesus answered, "What is born of the flesh is flesh, and what is born of the Spirit is spirit" (John 3:4, 6).

We are more than flesh and blood. By flesh and blood, we are born into the natural body, but it is the inner being—the spirit and the members of the triangles—that makes us who we are. The natural body depends on natural resources for existence and reproduction. In the same way, the spiritual body needs spiritual food, and the Spirit gives birth to spirit. Love gives birth to love and hate gives birth to hate. The Spirit of God is a transformative power. When we choose to love God, we connect our spirits with God's Spirit, and we enjoy that relationship. In this relationship, God adopts us as His children. The door to God's house is always open, and there is always a seat for us at His table. It is our choice whether we claim our heritage, enter God's house, and eat and drink with the family of God.

PRAYER:
Thank you, Lord, for loving me and adopting me as Your child.
Help me choose to love You always and not run away from Your presence.
Help me not to neglect the spiritual food or find a cheap substitute for it.
Grant me spiritual hunger so that I will come to Your table for nourishment.
Amen.

Visualize that you are sitting at a table with family and friends, having a good meal and enjoyable conversation. Now, visualize that you are there at the invitation of a friend, and that the friend is Jesus.

Believe today you will be salt of the earth and light of the world.

DAY TWELVE

Indeed, the word of God is living and active, sharper than any two-edged sword, piercing until it divides soul from spirit, joints from marrow; it is able to judge the thoughts and intentions of the heart.
HEBREWS 4:12

The Word of God is power. It is the creative power that brought forth the universe and all within it. The creative power of God took on flesh and blood and was born as a human child in a manger. Jesus was God's creative power in action. However, Jesus—a person of flesh and blood—had to use God's Word against temptations. Jesus used the Word of God as a double-edged sword; God's Word acted as a defensive weapon to resist temptation and as an offensive weapon to drive away the tempter. Temptations divide the mind, but the Word of God settles the mind and gives it direction to follow God's will.

The Word of God is an invisible, sharp, double-edged, spiritual sword. It gives an edge over all the destructive powers that work within our spirits. When we face temptation, God's Word acts as the discerning power of God, and when we are confused, God's Word acts as the guiding power of God. It is the reviving power of God when we are in despair, the healing power of God when we are sick, and the loving power of God when we feel hate. Yes, the Word of God is the very presence of God that brings peace to every troubled heart.

The Word of God is His promissory note for me.
I will bank on it for as long as I live, for I am a child of God.
The Word of God is the inexhaustible power of God for me.
So I will plug into it and draw energy for my daily journey.

The Word of God is the power of light in my darkness.
It will shine through the darkest night leading my path to light.
The Word of God assures me of my Savior's guiding presence;
I meditate on it day and night and enjoy the fullness of life.

PRAYER:
Dear Lord, let Your Word empower me today to follow the path of righteousness and peace. May Your Word fill my heart with the power of love, peace, and joy, and may it guide me from darkness and to your light. Amen.

Meditate on your favorite Scriptures all day and visualize the presence of God. Commit yourself to speak only positive words today.

Believe today you will be salt of the earth and light of the world.

DAY THIRTEEN

But he said to me, "My grace is sufficient for you,
for power is made perfect in weakness."
2 CORINTHIANS 12:9

The Apostle Paul, a well-educated Jewish scholar, did not experience the closeness of God and the intimate presence of the Holy Spirit through his strict observance of the law. Only through Jesus Christ did Paul find amazing power and intimate fellowship. He testified that God did not answer his prayer as he requested, but he received a promise: the gift of grace and power. With these gifts, Paul had an amazing experience. He said, "For whenever I am weak, then I am strong" (2 Corinthians 12:10). How can this be?

Has your car failed to start because of a weak car battery? You then must use jumper cables and channel enough power from a good battery into the weak battery to start the car. When you face problems that sap your energy, God's grace is your jumper cable that channels power from above. When you are full of sorrow and your inner being is downcast, God's grace is the cable that connects your soul to the power of God. When you feel that you have come to the end of the road and the world has shut itself against you, the grace of God leads the way and opens new possibilities. When you are criticized and your adversaries seek to destroy your self-esteem, Jesus Christ is the cable that recharges your inner being to face the world with courage and confidence.

Connect your inner triangle (mind) with the immeasurable, inexhaustible, incredible power of God. God is the triangle consisting of Father, Son, and Holy Spirit. Let the energy flow from the inner triangle to the outer triangle (God's Spirit to human mind) and balance the angles of your triangles. Draw power from the creative source. Draw power every day for your body, soul, and mind. Draw power from above to balance all the members of your triangles.

PRAYER:
Lord, please connect me with Your Holy Spirit so that I can draw Your power for my weakness and Your strength to climb the mountains of impossibilities. Amen.

Invoke the grace of God and visualize the Spirit of God surrounding your triangles with grace to face all situations today.

Believe today you will be salt of the earth and light of the world.

DAY FOURTEEN

Praise the Lord! O give thanks to the Lord, for he is good;
for his steadfast love endures forever.
PSALM 106:1

God is good all the time. Giving thanks connects our inner beings with the Spirit of God. God the Creator stopped the act of creating on the seventh day and rested. This is the example we should follow. This example comes from a loving Father to His children. We can keep working every hour of every day. We may be pressed to finish a task or to begin a new one. We may be pressured to make a higher wage by working extended hours, or to make a hard living by working overtime. No matter what, we should stop working to rest and rejuvenate our earthly bodies. We are taken out of the dust, the perishable elements of nature. We must respect the need for rest within our bodies. Resist the temptations to work on the Lord's Day (Sunday). Give rest to the body, which will bring calmness to the mind and enrichment to the spirit.

On the Lord's Day, give thanks to God. Join with fellow believers in worship, praise, and thanksgiving to God. Connect your inner being with the Spirit and the power of God. Please do not be anxious, but rather trust God's strength for your unfinished work.

In the morning, I see God's faithfulness by the rising sun.
In nature, I see God's faithfulness in the growing grass.
In the sky, I see God's faithfulness in the moving clouds.
In the night, I see God's faithfulness in the stars above.

I trust in God as I give rest to my body, soul, and mind.
I will sing praises to my God, who gives me strength every day.
I will praise God in the company of people who seek the Lord.
I will rejoice in the Lord, my Creator, Savior, and strength.

PRAYER:
Lord, please remove all anxieties from my mind so that I will be able to worship You in Spirit and in truth. May your Spirit enrich, empower, and fill my inner being with love, peace, and joy. Amen.

Relax and meditate on the goodness of the Lord. Recite a melody, chorus, or verse of a song of thanksgiving to God. Believe that God can provide for all your needs and relax.

Believe today you will be salt of the earth and light of the world.

DAY FIFTEEN

Blessed are the poor in spirit, for theirs is the kingdom of heaven.
MATTHEW 5:3

"Blessed" is a state of mind. However, people often associate blessings with material prosperity and wealth. In a political campaign, a presidential candidate said that he is blessed in that he can pay his taxes. He associates the concept of blessings with having plenty of money.

We associate not only wealth but also fame and reputation with being blessed. On the other hand, Jesus said that being poor is the state of being blessed. Jesus was not referring to material things, but the spirit. Being poor in spirit, therefore, is a state of mind, a state of wanting and needing more. Perhaps Jesus had the peasants of Galilee in mind. In the eyes of the religious scholars, they were the "flocks of the soil." In the eyes of the learned, the poorer populations were ignorant. In the eyes of the civilized, they were "backward." These people were unsophisticated, simple people. They were willing to learn and grow. They manifested a gentle spirit within them.

The opposite of the "poor in spirit" is the "prideful in spirit." It is an attitude of "I know it all" and "I have it all." This attitude leaves little room for dialogue, growth, and change. In pride, there is no simplicity, compassion, or seeing the needs of one's neighbors. In this prideful state, members of the triangles do not submit to God's Spirit.

One day, a rich, young ruler came to Jesus and asked him, "Good Teacher, what must I do to inherit eternal life?" He further stated that he had followed religious teachings since he was young. Jesus told him, "Sell all that you own and distribute the money to the poor, and you will have treasure in heaven; then come, follow me" (Luke 18:18, 22). The gospel writer then tells us that the young man was extremely disappointed upon hearing this because he had many possessions. He left Jesus, unable to make the commitment to follow Him.

Being poor in spirit is to humbly submit our spirits to God's Spirit. It means to bring all our knowledge and everything we have within us to Jesus Christ, allowing the Spirit of God to balance the triangles of our inner beings. Being poor in spirit calls us to remove self-centered thoughts and replace them with God's love.

PRAYER:
Gentle Savior, come into my inner being and help me remove the pride, hate, prejudice, and all other destructive spirits from within. Fill me with Your Spirit of love so that I will be Your disciple today and every day. Amen.

Visualize the cleansing Spirit of God from the inner triangle moving toward your outer triangles, washing away the accumulated stains caused by unholy and prideful thoughts.

Believe today you will be salt of the earth and light of the world.

DAY SIXTEEN

Blessed are those who mourn, for they will be comforted.
MATTHEW 5:4

This verse appears to be a contradiction. If it is not a contradiction, then it is a paradox, hard to understand. Is not mourning an expression of pain and anguish, a state of the curse? If so, then why did Jesus make such a statement?

Mourning, or lamentation, should be understood in two different ways. First, it is pain affected by the evils of the world. No one is entirely protected from the evils in our world. In the Old Testament, there was an undertone that the righteous would not suffer evil. The book of Job reveals this concept. Job's friends tried to convince him that the pain and evil he suffered from was because of his sins. Job did not give in to that idea and stood firm in his belief that he did not deserve such pain. When God addressed this issue, He rebuked Job's friends and told them that Job's sins had not brought suffering upon him. God then told Job not to question God's power and integrity. Paul the Apostle wrote in his letter to the Romans, "And not only that, but we also boast in our sufferings, knowing that suffering produces endurance, and endurance produces character, and character produces hope, and hope does not disappoint us, because God's love has been poured into our hearts through the Holy Spirit that has been given to us" (Romans 5:3–5).

Mourning is a lamentation for our sins. It is the sincere attitude of repentance. When we repent of sin and turn to God, we experience the pain of dispossessing negative emotions. These could be long-kept anger, hate, prejudice, and other destructive forces we have been holding on to. Repentance is often a purposeful process of removing the clutter that inhibits our inner beings. It denies the emotions and sinful desires of the flesh. The Apostle Paul said that he died daily for the sake of Christ. To repent means to practice spiritual discipline and follow Jesus as Lord and Master. It is upon sorrowful repentance that we experience the joy of God's comfort.

PRAYER:
Dear Lord, remove the fears of mourning and give me faith that I will rejoice in You. Fill my heart with Your love so that I will reach out and touch those who are mourning and offer them comfort and hope. Amen.

Visualize the comforting presence of God's Spirit filling your inner being with joy. Seek to comfort someone today.

Believe today you will be salt of the earth and light of the world.

DAY SEVENTEEN

Blessed are the meek, for they will inherit the earth.
MATTHEW 5:5

We often associate meekness with weakness. Meekness is an attitude born of God's Spirit. To be meek means to show goodwill toward fellow humans and to show reverence toward God. Meekness allows the Holy Spirit to work over our self-centered spirits so that action does not become aggression, the opposite of meekness.

Acts of aggression interfere with the freedom of others. Throughout history, we find a string of aggressors intent on possessing land and living eternally. We may remember a few names: Alexander the Great, Napoleon, and Hitler. We might remember a few kingdoms like Rome, Greece, and Great Britain. They all were once aggressive powers that now remain only as fading memories.

However, Jesus was meek, and He told His disciples not to take a sword against their enemies, even in self-defense. When Jesus died, He did not have anything to call His own, yet He remains the most admired person in human history.

Meekness allows God's Spirit to control all the members of the triangles and shows submission to the Spirit of God. A meek person is mindful of others' rights and does not interfere with, disturb, or hurt others. Meekness removes the possibilities that stem from aggressive thoughts and actions. However, that does not mean a meek person will give in to other pressures or give up because of pressures. A meek person is purposeful in whatever he or she does. They possess strength, courage, and character.

PRAYER:
Fill my soul, dear Lord, not with pride but with humility.
Fill my inner being with the spirit of meekness, I pray.
Fill my soul with the Spirit of Jesus, who stood before Pilate.
Fill it fully so that I will not let temptations divide my soul.
Fill my heart with Your Spirit, dear Lord.
Fill it with meekness that I will not hurt another.
Fill it with courage that I will not be afraid of the world.
Fill it, Lord; fill it every day so that I will stand firm for You. Amen.

Visualize the presence of God in your soul and practice kindness toward others.

Believe today you will be salt of the earth and light of the world.

DAY EIGHTEEN

Blessed are those who hunger and thirst for righteousness, for they will be filled.
MATTHEW 5:6

To be righteous is to be just. It is to be wholesome in thoughts and just in actions. Righteousness allows God's Spirit to lead the mind for action. None of us should think that we will always follow the will of God and be righteous just because we have accepted Jesus Christ as Lord and Savior, we are baptized, and we attend worship services. Each one of these steps should condition our inner beings to be obedient to God's Holy Spirit and to be righteous.

Physical hunger is a natural reminder of the body's need. Without physical hunger, creatures would not eat. Just like physical hunger turns our attention toward food, spiritual hunger turns our hearts toward God's Spirit. When we are full of food, our appetites are limited, perhaps only for dessert. This same principle applies to spiritual hunger. When the inner being is full of unholy thoughts, desires, ambitions, lust, pleasure, greed, prejudice, and other negative forces, we do not have room for spiritual food. Christians often take spiritual food like dessert, eating it after a full meal. Some people push dessert away because they have had too much to eat. Others who take a bite soon forget its taste.

Very seldom do most Americans experience deep hunger or thirst. If this is true about physical food and drink, it is true about spiritual food, too. Therefore, we must be purposeful about spiritual food. To become spiritually hungry and to have a genuine appetite for spiritual food, we must lower our intake of junk food; we must empty our minds of every defiling thought and become hungry for God's food. Remove all fears from your mind—fear of pain, fear of rejection and loneliness, fear of ill health and death. Remove all lust, adulterous fantasy, greed, and evil desires. Empty your thoughts of all prejudices toward different ethnicities, individuals, groups, vocations, and cultures. Seek to become like a child. It will not be easy, but it is possible. Now, ask God to bring all your triangles in harmony and fill your inner being with unconditional love.

PRAYER:
Loving God, fill me with spiritual food today so that I will have the energy to do the right actions and be righteous in Your sight. Grant me spiritual hunger every day so that I will seek after Your righteousness. Amen.

Meditate on your favorite scripture and pray that God will use you as an instrument of His righteousness.

Believe today you will be salt of the earth and light of the world.

DAY NINETEEN

Blessed are the merciful, for they will receive mercy.
MATTHEW 5:7

A person who seeks to follow God's righteousness must be filled with God's love. The fullness of love brings forth grace, which then results in mercy. Love is like a plant that grows and blooms to produce fruit.

First, the inner being must have room for God's love and must desire to be filled with God's love. It must become stronger to control the thought processes. The Apostle Paul said that we are to "take every thought captive to obey Christ" (2 Corinthians 10:5). This cannot and will not happen automatically. We must practice spiritual discipline to allow God's love to become stronger than self-love.

Secondly, when God's love becomes stronger, we then act on love. A few things become natural. Like a parent holding a child, loving becomes a natural part of the Christian life. When a child expresses free will in the form of disobedience, loving becomes a conscious act. At this stage in parenting, expressions of love are not always easy. This stage calls for discipline. Discipline becomes important for both the parent and the child. When the child disobeys, there should be grace from the parents. When the child deserves punishment, there should be mercy. Because the parent-child relationship is a unique, possessive love, the two seek to maintain a relationship. In a conflict in a relationship with a stranger, we feel no investment in the stranger and give up. However, God's love will not give up.

Thirdly, God's love is different from our love. God's love is unconditional and full of mercy. While we were sinners, Christ died for us. That is unconditional love. Mercy is the act of not punishing one according to what they deserve. Mercy is the act of love with grace. Love without action is powerless. God's love must fill our minds; we must desire to act with love as God would act in that situation, and the result is being merciful. Grace is the overflowing love of God that enables us to practice mercy.

PRAYER:
Dear Lord, help me practice spiritual discipline so that I will act on love. Fill me with Your love so that I will manifest Your grace and act on Your behalf in mercy. In Jesus's name I pray, Amen.

Think of a situation in which you were the recipient of mercy, and then look for an opportunity to be merciful.

Believe today you will be salt of the earth and light of the world.

DAY TWENTY

Blessed are the pure in heart, for they will see God.
MATTHEW 5:8

What does it mean to be "pure in heart"? According to the Bible, the heart represents the whole personality. It involves the thoughts that lead to emotions. The heart also includes all accumulated information in the mind. To be pure is to not have anything that defiles, corrupts, or makes us unclean. Pure gold has gone through fire to melt away any defiling materials. Therefore, "pure in heart" describes a personality that has removed all defiling thoughts and allows the Holy Spirit full control. In this person, nothing corrupts, inhibits, or hinders fellowship with God.

Christians must have singleness of heart. Jesus pointed out, "Strive first for the kingdom of God and his righteousness" (Matthew 6:33). This should be the first and foremost objective of God's people. God's kingdom cannot come without God's righteousness. God's righteousness cannot become a reality in the world without God's people. God's people cannot create God's reality without giving their hearts to Him. Giving our hearts to God is more than a verbal affirmation. We must practice spiritual disciplines that allow God to guide us and bring all our triangles into harmony. We should welcome God's Spirit into the center of our inner beings as a permanent resident.

Without spiritual discipline, we are blind to God. Those who want to become rich focus on success and create a god out of success. Those who follow the desires of the carnal mind focus on the gods of sex and lust. Jesus said, "No one has ever seen God. It is God the only Son, who is close to the Father's heart, who has made him known" (John 1:18). Jesus revealed God to us. Jesus told Philip, one of His disciples, that "whoever has seen me has seen the Father" (John 14:9). Jesus did not simply mean His flesh and blood, but rather the Spirit of God within Him. We must have spiritual eyes to see God. We must have spiritual ears to hear God, and we must have spiritual minds to commune with God. The world around us may be blind, but we can see God. We can enter His presence, and we can commune with God every day, every hour, and every moment.

PRAYER:
Dear Lord, I submit all the angles of my triangles to you. Help me focus on You and see You clearly. Please come and dwell in my heart so that I will commune with You this day and every day. Amen.

Visualize the cleansing power of the Holy Spirit removing every defiling thought from your mind, keeping your angles in balance.

Believe today you will be salt of the earth and light of the world.

DAY TWENTY-ONE

Blessed are the peacemakers, for they will be called children of God.
MATTHEW 5:9

Children of God not only affirm faith in Jesus Christ but also do God's will. They represent God in their world. They are peacemakers. Loving peace and making peace are different. Making peace means to bring God's love in action to a troubling situation.

To be peacemakers, we must experience peace within. To experience perfect peace, all our triangles should be balanced, and all members of the angles should work together. Peace allows God's Spirit to remove friction. Peace wills the spirit to let go and let God, to give up inhibitions and let go of prejudice, anger, misunderstanding, and other root causes of troubles that war within our inner beings. The war should be over, and the peace treaty must be signed within our souls. God's Holy Spirit should remain as a permanent peacekeeper in our hearts.

Peacemaking makes hostile people hospitable. Peacemaking is the Christian mission, and we must carry out our mission as God's children. The people of the world often return hostility with hostility, but God's children must react to hostility with hospitality. God's children may sometimes appear weak, and even cowardly, in the eyes of the world. However, God's children should have their purpose in mind; they should not keep up with the standards or expectations of the world but should do God's will. Christians aim to be disciples of Jesus, Who, in all situations, seeks to redeem people. They are purposeful in building friendships.

The enemy may be a hostile person who seeks to destroy you. The enemies of Jesus crucified His body, but they could not kill His soul and Spirit. When we reach out to love our enemies, we must believe in God's mighty power. In most situations of peacemaking, we will see the transforming power of God changing lives. We must be purposeful in our task as disciples of Jesus and wear the hidden nametag, "Peacemaker." Peace must manifest in our words and actions.

PRAYER:
Dear Lord, please help me to be a peacemaker. Let the words of my mouth diffuse a quarrel, mend a broken relationship, and heal a wounded heart. Amen.

Keep your angles balanced and visualize the Spirit of God leading you to be a peacemaker.

Believe today you will be salt of the earth and light of the world.

DAY TWENTY-TWO

Blessed are those who are persecuted for righteousness' sake,
for theirs is the kingdom of heaven.
MATTHEW 5:10

The kingdom of heaven belongs not only to those who are "poor in spirit" but also to those who are persecuted for the sake of righteousness. How sad it is that people hurt people. Unfortunately, that is reality. Today, Americans are not persecuted for our religious beliefs as the first-century Christians were. We cherish individual freedom and democracy. However, we can and do hurt one another because of our likes and dislikes, fears and prejudices, greed, and lust. We must disarm internal friction to stop external friction. We must consider our inner struggles to bring all members of the triangles under submission to God's Spirit as our persecution for following the path of righteousness. It is not easy to give up the prejudices that inhibit our inner beings, but we must follow the courageous people who set examples of righteousness.

Jesus pointed out that the prophets of God were courageous people who advocated God's righteousness at the expense of their lives. The prophets suffered pain, and even death, for the sake of God's righteousness. Their enemies hated them. It is fortunate that our enemies are not people seeking to kill us but are instead the members of our inner beings. When we accept Jesus Christ as our Lord and Master, we surrender all members of our inner beings to God. We are no longer controlled by the members of the triangles, but by the Spirit of God. The members of our triangles are no longer enslaved by inhibitions but are empowered to follow the mission of Christ. When we love God with our entire inner beings, we then focus on God's righteousness. God wants all His children to work for righteousness. If we are afraid to give up our inhibitions, we will fail. We must change our thinking and believe in the power of God. We must invoke the presence of God and draw creative energy to overcome inhibitions and frictions from within. Only then will we produce the fruit of righteousness.

PRAYER:
Loving God, please remove the fears that limit my ability to serve you and fill my heart with courage. Help me to follow Your will and bring Your righteousness into my inner being and into my world. Amen.

Visualize the Spirit of God as the captain of your inner being and envision all members of the triangles obeying orders and working together.

Believe today you will be salt of the earth and light of the world.

DAY TWENTY-THREE

*You are the salt of the earth; but if salt has lost its taste, how can
its saltiness be restored? It is no longer good for anything,
but is thrown out and trampled under foot.*
MATTHEW 5:13

Remember Jesus's teaching in Matthew chapter thirteen about "making a tree good"? Think of it as a spiritual grafting method. This is the work of the Holy Spirit, the creative energy. Allowing the Holy Spirit into our lives helps us participate in the Spirit of God as Jesus participated in the Spirit of the heavenly Father. How does this become a reality in the life of the believer? By placing the Word of God in our thought processes and allowing the Spirit of God to take charge. Jesus said in the book of Luke that out of the overflow of the heart, the mouth speaks. Godly thoughts will bring forth the best of attitudes and actions. Indeed, the person who has the Spirit of God will make a positive difference in his world. The followers of Jesus have the Spirit of God. Jesus will become a reality in His followers through the indwelling presence of the Holy Spirit. Therefore, believers are called to do the work of Jesus: they are to be salt.

There were many uses for salt in Jesus's world. In semi-tropical Palestine, salt preserved food, added flavor to food, healed wounds, and stopped decay. The qualities of salt must manifest through the lives of God's children. With the Spirit of God within, believers can add good taste to their world. They are also able to touch any decaying elements and cure them.

Christians can do the work of God as salt. We can add saltiness with a gentle smile against the bitterness of a frown, bring hope in despair, and bring peace in times of trouble. We can bring the healing touch of understanding against the decay of prejudice, and we can remove the bitterness of indifference toward our neighbors and build friendships. Christians are positive people. We draw our saltiness from the Spirit of God and gently pass it on to our world.

PRAYER:
Loving God, fill me with Your saltiness so that I will bring forth the best taste and healing in my world. Make me an agent of transformation in Your world today and every day. Amen.

Believe and visualize God using you to bring positive changes into the world in which you live.

Believe today you will be salt of the earth and light of the world.

DAY TWENTY-FOUR

You are the light of the world. A city built on a hill cannot be hid.
No one after lighting a lamp puts it under the bushel basket,
but on the lampstand, and it gives light to all in the house.
In the same way, let your light shine before others, so that they
may see your good works and give glory to your Father in heaven.
MATTHEW 5:14–16

The world needs more than sunshine and moonlight to see the way, understand the truth, and receive the fullness of life. Followers of Jesus know that Jesus is the way, the truth, and the life. They are the participants of the fullness of life and are responsible for bringing God's light into their world. The light of Jesus must shine through them. Just as sunshine starts the process of photosynthesis in plants, Christians must radiate God's righteousness into their world to bring forth spiritual transformation in the hearts of other people. Without the Light of God's Spirit, people will die from spiritual malnutrition.

In the above passage from Matthew, Jesus said, "No one after lighting a lamp puts it under the bushel basket, but on the lampstand." Christians are called to do the mission of Christ, to bring forth God's light into our world. Just like the moon shines in darkness by reflecting the sun's light, Christians must radiate God's light into the darkness of the world. As the moonlight gently leads the way to dawn, Christians should gently lead those who are in darkness to Jesus, God's greater light. The moon shines throughout the night, not by its own energy, but by the sun's energy. Christians can and should shed light in darkness: not by our own strength, but by God's power within us.

O Jesus, come into my heart and remove the darkness of my soul.

O Jesus, shine forth Your light through my words and deeds.

Shine, Jesus, that Your light will shine through me today.

Shine, Jesus, that the world will see Your way.

PRAYER:
Dear Lord, fill my thoughts with Your presence so that all members of my inner being will produce the fruit of righteousness and radiate Your light in my words, attitudes, and actions. Fill me full of Your love so that I will bring forth Your light into my world. Amen.

Believe and visualize that you are a participant of the Light of God. You are becoming a person of God's influence upon others.

Believe today you will be salt of the earth and light of the world.

DAY TWENTY-FIVE

Do not think that I have come to abolish the law or the prophets;
I have not come to abolish them but to fulfill them.
MATTHEW 5:17, NIV

Dear Lord, I present myself to you today. I call myself a Christian to follow You all the way. I read your words; I say my prayers; I go to church to be with fellow believers, and I remember Your death by the sacraments. What else do you want me to do, dear Lord?

Give Me your inner being, says the Spirit of God. *Give Me your anxious thoughts and trust Me. Look at the sky above and put your trust in Me. Look closely at the hills and see My handiwork. Who moves the clouds that travel far and wide? Who pours out rain to the thirsty ground and makes the rivers flow? Who makes the flowers grow in the pastureland? Who has assigned colors and shapes to them? Do not trust in your own righteousness, but be in communion with Me.*

God is good, God alone is powerful to set the earth in motion.
God is good, God alone is the commander of life on earth.
God is good, God alone is wiser, Who created human beings.
God is good, God alone is the source of all creation.

Commune with your Creator, O my soul.
Commune in the Spirit of the Master who lived in Galilee.
Hear Him speak the words, "Do not be anxious."
Hear Him call you to give your inner beings in submission.

TALK TO THE MASTER AND TELL HIM:
"Take my life and let it be consecrated, Lord, to thee . . .
Take my hands and let them move at the impulse of thy love . . .
Take my love; my Lord, I pour at thy feet its treasure store.
Take myself, and I will be ever, only, all for thee.
Ever, only, all for thee. Amen."[23]

Meditate within your inner being on the goodness of the Lord and fill your mind with loving thoughts.

Believe today you will be salt of the earth and light of the world.

DAY TWENTY-SIX

*For I tell you, unless your righteousness exceeds that of the scribes
and Pharisees, you will never enter the kingdom of heaven.*
MATTHEW 5:20

The scribes were the religious teachers of the law. They were educated, religious lawyers of Jesus's day who were highly esteemed. They protected the law, expounded the Old Testament laws, and administered them as jurists.

The Pharisees were the most visibly religious people in Jesus's time. They separated themselves from the "evils of the world" and disassociated themselves from people who did not follow the strict religious rules of the day. The Pharisees were careful in practicing religious observances, meticulous in their giving, and charitable toward the poor. They were patriotic and pious, often wearing long robes to identify with conservative religious groups. Why, then, did Jesus not admire them and instead highlight them as a warning sign of "not enough"?

Why did Jesus call His followers to standards higher than those of the Pharisees and the teachers of the law? They sought outward righteousness rather than inward righteousness. Jesus pointed to them as white-washed tombs; while the tomb appeared clean outside, it decayed inside. Jesus called for inward change, inward righteousness, and inward holiness.

Jesus called for God's righteousness within the hearts of His followers before they promoted God's righteousness to others. This was a different approach from that of the scribes and Pharisees. Jesus's followers were called not to seek the praise of others, but to practice the spiritual principles within one's own heart. Jesus's teaching called for more than obedience to the law. He called His followers to understand the spirit of the law and to practice it enthusiastically. The Apostle Paul said, "The letter kills, but the Spirit gives life" (2 Corinthians 3:6). It was more than knowledge. It was the Spirit of God that brought forth God's righteousness into action. The followers of Jesus are called to be true to themselves within their inner beings.

PRAYER:
Lord, remove from me every desire of praise from others. Make me a servant today, dear Lord, a servant of love, unconditional love. Help me to follow You and learn from You this day and every day. Amen.

Practice God's holiness within your inner being and do an act of kindness, not for recognition, but out of the goodness of your heart.

Believe today you will be salt of the earth and light of the world.

DAY TWENTY-SEVEN

You have heard that it was said to those of ancient times,
"You shall not murder"; and "whoever murders shall be liable to judgment."
But I say to you that if you are angry with a brother or sister, you will be liable
to the council; and if you insult a brother or sister, you will be liable to the
council; and if you say, "You fool," you will be liable to hell.
MATTHEW 5:21–22

Jesus called His followers to a higher standard. He pointed out the standards of the world—of the religious community, Pharisees, and scribes—and said, "This is not enough." You must surpass the world's standards to practice God's righteousness and be the salt of the earth and the light of the world. What is the higher standard of Jesus? It is the standard of the Spirit.

Murder is not only an act of the hands; it is also an act of the mind. The world sees and judges only the outward action, but God sees and judges the inward thoughts. The root cause of murder and other such violence is anger, an emotion. Unchecked anger produces evil plots against one's adversaries. Jesus said that our words come out of our thoughts. When our thoughts are controlled by anger, God is not in control. Anger is a destructive emotion and brings out the worst from within us. When we eliminate the power of anger from our inner beings, we will eliminate violence.

Take inventory of your inner being and see yourself in God's presence. Have you ever wished your enemy dead? Have you stabbed a person, not with knives, but with words? Have you raised your voice to subdue an opponent? We all, at one time or another, have fallen short of God's glory. However, sin should not rule us. Anger should not control our inner beings. Practice self-discipline and overcome the power of anger. It will help you experience the power of God in practical situations.

PRAYER:
When my thoughts are tense with anger, calm my soul, dear Lord.
Whenever I am about to say a hateful word in anger, speak to my soul.
When I hate my enemy and would like to utter a harsh word, stop my tongue.
Remove thoughts of anger and tension from my inner being, I pray. Amen.

See yourself as a balanced triangle who does not allow destructive emotions to control your mind.

Believe today you will be salt of the earth and light of the world.

DAY TWENTY-EIGHT

So when you are offering your gift at the altar, if you remember
that your brother or sister has something against you, leave your gift
there before the altar and go; first be reconciled to your
brother or sister, and then come and offer your gift.
MATTHEW 5:23–24

Offering gifts at the altar represents worship. Worship is more than giving gifts to God. Worship is drawing closer to God's Spirit. Jesus said, "God is spirit, and his worshippers must worship in spirit and in truth" (John 4:24). To worship is to invite God's Spirit into our inner triangles, which must be in harmony with the Spirit of God. The Apostle John pointed out the differences between the children of God and the children of the devil: "And by this we will know that we are from the truth and will reassure our hearts before him whenever our hearts condemn us; for God is greater than our hearts, and he knows everything" (1 John 3:19–20). God is greater than our conscious and subconscious minds. God is greater than our rational minds and all rationalizations. No number of sacrifices will repair broken relationships.

How can a bullet hit the target when the scope is not set? The scope must be fixed to hit the target. When our inner triangles are not set correctly and are not guided by God's Spirit, our offerings will not connect with God's Spirit. To the rich and the wealthy, God said, "I will not accept a bull from your house, or goats from your folds" (Psalm 50:9).

King David understood it and uttered, "A broken and contrite heart, O God, you will not despise" (Psalm 51:17). In worship, we should not hide our hearts behind loud music. When we hear the preaching of God's Word, we should not look for loopholes for our unrepentant souls. In the loving call to communion with our Master, we must examine our hearts. No escape should be given to the restless mind until it repents and repairs that relationship with fellow human beings. The cleansed inner being receives the unhindered flow of God's energy within. This is true worship: communion with the Spirit of our Lord and Master.

PRAYER:
Dear Lord, help me commune with You today. Let the words of my mouth and the meditations of my heart be acceptable to You, this day and every day. Amen.

Think of God's love and grace for you. Offer God the gift of thanksgiving. Let your inner being overflow with gratitude for your Savior.

Believe today you will be salt of the earth and light of the world.

DAY TWENTY-NINE

*You have heard that it was said, "You shall not commit adultery."
But I say to you that everyone who looks at a woman with lust has already
committed adultery with her in his heart. If your right eye causes you to sin,
tear it out and throw it away; it is better for you to lose one of your members
than for your whole body to be thrown into hell. And if your right hand
causes you to sin, cut it off and throw it away; it is better for you to lose
one of your members than for your whole body to go into hell.*
MATTHEW 5:27–30

Sexual fantasies and infatuations are normal for the human mind. Christianity does not deny the joy of romance; rather, it promotes romance throughout married life. However, Christianity does not give room for adultery, fornication, and other such sexual behaviors. Sexual infidelity destroys marriages and families, bringing pain and suffering.

Look at our culture. We see sex appeal everywhere. It is on billboards, newspapers, radio, and television. Sex is a successful marketing tool in our culture. Without much elaboration, we can admit that we live in a sex-crazed culture. In this society, people are prompted to think lustfully. We are challenged to go after pleasure and ignore moral values.

Christians are called to live above the world's standards. Within the inner being of a Christian, romance for one's spouse should be stronger than the beguiling love of another person. According to Jesus, adultery is not only a physical act but also a mental one. The carnal mind defiles an individual's thinking by promoting thoughts of lust, which is the act of the flesh. Lust is not born of God's love, but of self. Unchecked lust grows faster than the fastest cancer cells and destroys one's true love and commitment to their spouse. When it came to adultery and lust, Jesus called for physical mutilation to save one from the condemnation of hell. Living above the world's standards means that we must funnel every thought through the Spirit of God and remove the defiling thoughts of lust. This is not an easy task, but it is possible.

PRAYER:
Loving Master, remove lustful thoughts from my heart. Grant me the courage to cut off every relationship that promotes lust within my heart. Amen.

In your heart, limit sexual fantasies toward only your spouse and invoke God's holiness against every defiling thought.

Believe today you will be salt of the earth and light of the world.

DAY THIRTY

Let your word be "Yes, yes" or "No, no";
anything more than this comes from the evil one.
MATTHEW 5:37

Why does a person swear? Isn't it a calling to a higher authority to authenticate his words? Christians are always under a higher authority, and we should not forget that. Christians are always under the watchful eye of the Holy Spirit, and we should not ignore that. Perhaps others may not see and highlight your faults, but God sees them, and God's Holy Spirit attributes your faults to the morals of your inner triangle.

How do you live, act, and conduct yourself when no one is looking? Your behavior behind closed doors is the real indication of who you are. To be a Christian in all situations is to be honest in all situations. A child of God leaves no room for dishonesty. We are not scrutinized by the world's standards, but by a higher standard of the Holy Spirit. As children of God, we should not allow dark or gray areas in our lives. We are not to give room to cunning, craftiness, deception, or other questionable acts. Christians must seek to live above reproach.

The evil of dishonesty blocks the flow of God's creative energy. Removing dishonesty from our minds and replacing it with honesty is the first step in allowing God's Spirit to take control of our inner beings. When we do this, we remove a burden from our backs or remove a tumor from our bodies. Peace, joy, and abundant life are possible only when we remove everything that hinders the flow of God's Spirit within our inner beings. As children of God, we must be 100 percent honest with ourselves. Do not leave in the mind any room for deception or dishonesty. When you do not give control to the members of your angles, but to God's Spirit, you can fully practice the virtue of honesty.

PRAYER:
Remove from my mind every deceptive inhibition, I pray.
Fill my thoughts with courage and character that I will be faithful.
Let my words be wholesome and true in all situations of life.
Let not my desires but Your Spirit be in control of my mind, I pray. Amen.

Affirm to your mind, "I will be true to God's Spirit, and I will practice truthfulness all of the time, for I am a child of God."

Believe today you will be salt of the earth and light of the world.

DAY THIRTY-ONE

It was also said, "Whoever divorces his wife, let him give her a certificate of divorce." But I say to you that anyone who divorces his wife, except on the ground of unchastity, causes her to commit adultery; and whoever marries a divorced woman commits adultery.

MATTHEW 5:31–32

The religious teachers of Jesus's day questioned Him on more than one occasion about divorce. A Pharisee pointed out that Moses permitted divorce. Jesus responded, "It was because you were so hard-hearted that Moses allowed you to divorce your wives" (Matthew 19:8).

Marriage is more than a ceremony and more than the recitation of wedding vows. It is the joining together of two hearts. It is a commitment between two individuals' inner beings that they will make their hearts work together for a lifetime. It is discipline. No marriage—regardless of how much money, religion, children, or other things are involved—will remain strong, true, and fulfilling without oneness of heart. Christian spouses must practice spiritual discipline and remove any hindrances from their hearts to become one in their everyday lives. It is a blessed union when both spouses regularly examine their inner beings to keep their angles in harmony with the Spirit of God. This regular examination removes the chances of unwanted pain and sorrow, misunderstandings and heartaches, infidelity, broken marriages, and broken homes.

When a couple grows apart without the guidance of the Holy Spirit, they experience hurt. However, if both spouses seek God's love to heal their relationship, God grants them the power of the Spirit to overcome the pain. When they follow spiritual discipline and practice unconditional love, their marriage becomes stronger and richer. They help each other to follow the path of righteousness and peace. Their inner beings are full of love and respect for each other. They do not have room in their minds to find fault with each other. The love of God—from their innermost triangles—empowers them to forgive the other's mistakes, faults, and failures. The love of God enables them to enjoy life together, and the two then build a strong, loving, fulfilling, and lasting relationship. They help each other to become their best.

PRAYER:
Loving God, let Your Spirit bring my heart together in love with my spouse's heart. Let us discover the power of Your love for our marriage. Amen.

In your mind, think only the most positive and loving thoughts toward your spouse. Seek ways to appreciate your spouse.

Believe today you will be salt of the earth and light of the world.

DAY THIRTY-TWO

You have heard that it was said, "An eye for an eye and
a tooth for a tooth." But I say to you, "Do not resist an evildoer.
But if anyone strikes you on the right cheek, turn the other also."
MATTHEW 5:38–39

How can we practice such a teaching? Of course, it is impossible with man, but all things are possible with God. If you were randomly picked to appear at the Super Bowl and told that you must kick a field goal of fifty yards to win a million dollars, could you do it? If you are a football player, you will try. If you played ball in school, you might give it a try. But how can a person who has never kicked a field goal ever hope to kick a football that far? It is impossible. This truth also applies to Christian living and spiritual discipline.

The teachings of Jesus, such as the verses above, are not easy to practice. However, they are possible. Athletes set new records because they practice overcoming their limitations. If physical exercise can train the physical body to set new records, spiritual discipline can train a believer and set new standards of behavior. It is possible, and we must believe this and work toward it.

Look to the example of Gandhi in his struggle for freedom for his country. He was not a professing Christian, but he loved the teachings of Jesus and applied them to his life. When Gandhi was booted down harshly by a British soldier, losing two of his teeth in the crushing impact, he was calm. He looked into the eyes of the soldier and asked him, "Brother, are you hurting?" Gandhi knew the soldier was merely obeying his orders, but Gandhi recognized that the soldier was a man with a soul, too. Gandhi saw the soldier's hurting soul beyond his own physical hurt. When we look at the world with the compassion of Christ, we will not be afraid of the insults we may suffer. Remember: "Greater is He who is in you than he that is in the world" (1 John 4:4, BSB).

PRAYER:
Dear Lord, fill me with Your compassion for the world and help me practice the spiritual principles so that I can follow Your teachings. Grant me courage so that I will reach out and touch with Your love even those who cause me pain. Amen.

Visualize the love of God filling your inner being so that your heart overflows with grace and greases the frictions within your relationships. You have the compassion to redeem those who hurt you.

Believe today you will be salt of the earth and light of the world.

DAY THIRTY-THREE

You have heard that it was said, "You shall love your neighbor
and hate your enemy." But I say to you, Love your enemies and pray
for those who persecute you, so that you may be children of your
Father in heaven; for he makes his sun rise on the evil and on the
good, and sends rain on the righteous and on the unrighteous.

MATTHEW 5:43–45

Love and hate are the two most compelling emotions in the human mind. For the fulfillment of love as romance, we forsake father, mother, brother, sister, and all other associations and attachments to cherish the love of our lover. Such love transcends religion, color, and culture. Real-life *Romeo and Juliet* stories play out between opposing cultures, such as when a Hindu and a Moslem fall in love and must keep their relationship a secret. Finding no way to cherish their love against the wishes of their families and their cultures, they hold on to each other as they jump to their deaths into the ocean. If love is such a great force within the spectrum of human emotion, what about hate?

Hate is a powerful emotion that draws a line between good and bad, right and wrong, friends and enemies. Hate toward people, especially a group of people, is not uncommon in many countries and cultures. The power of such hate occasionally raises its ugly head as murder. Hitler hated Jewish people, and the result of that hate was the terrible Holocaust. Other tragic hate crimes occur far too often, such as the ethnic cleansing in Rwanda, Bosnia, Kosovo, and other parts of the world. The Jews of Jesus's day were hateful toward the Samaritan people and the Romans.

Jesus called His disciples to undergo a transformation within their inner beings. They were commanded to love not only their friendly fellow Jewish people but also the Samaritans and the Romans, their perceived enemies. Jesus's disciples should not have any room for hate in their hearts. God is love, and in God there is no hate. We should not allow the members of our triangles to accumulate hateful information and build up power points in our minds. Whenever a thought of hate touches our emotions, we should not give room for it to dwell within the mind.

PRAYER:
Dear Lord, teach me to love those whom I do not like. Let the power of Your unconditional love flow through me this day and every day. Amen.

If you dislike someone, or you think another person or race of people dislikes you, ask God's love to take control of your inner being and visualize yourself loving everyone.

Believe today you will be salt of the earth and light of the world.

DAY THIRTY-FOUR

For if you love those who love you, what reward do you have? Do not even the tax collectors do the same? And if you greet only your brothers and sisters, what more are you doing than others? Do not even the Gentiles do the same? Be perfect, therefore, as your heavenly Father is perfect.
MATTHEW 5:46–48

Jesus calls His disciples to extraordinary living. They are neither like the average people of the world nor like the crowd. They are different because they have the indwelling Spirit of God keeping their angles in harmony. The disciples do not follow the standards of this world, but of a higher one: the world of the transforming power of God's love. It is by the practice of the transforming power of love they became the salt of the earth and the light of the world.

Jesus pointed out that it takes no spiritual discipline for us to love those who are lovable, but it takes a lot of discipline, courage, and character to love our enemies. Those who follow Jesus work toward God's righteousness and must practice radical obedience. The evils of the world will continue if we love only those who are lovable, but the disciples of Jesus will change the world by the power of the transforming love of God.

The world says hate your enemy; Jesus says love your enemy.

The world says hate your adversary; Jesus says pray for your adversary.

The world says fight your competition; Jesus says bless your competition.

The world says curse your opponent; Jesus says praise your opponent.

No one can practice such a radical change without practicing spiritual discipline. Jesus is our Lord. He is our Master Teacher Who says, "Follow me." We cannot practice spiritual discipline by our own power, but, by the power of God's love, we can practice it every day.

PRAYER:
Loving God, teach me to practice radical obedience and follow You every day. Fill my inner being with love and compassion so that I will reach out and touch those who are outside of my comfort zone. Amen.

Find something good in a person you dislike. Lift that person up to God and ask the Lord to bless that person. Pray that the Lord will fill your heart with great love for those who do not like you.

Believe today you will be salt of the earth and light of the world.

DAY THIRTY-FIVE

Beware of practicing your piety before others in order to be seen by them;
for then you have no reward from your Father in heaven.
MATTHEW 6:1

God, the Heavenly Father, knows the thoughts of our hearts. Our Heavenly Father knows the intentions and motives of our minds. The religion of Jesus is the religion of the inner being. It does not seek prideful admiration from others. It is not born out of false piety. No one can be greater than what is within their inner beings. Our inner beings are always open before God, and God alone is the true judge, who sees every angle within us. The psalmist said it correctly:

> "O Lord, you have searched me and known me. You know when I sit down and when I rise up; you discern my thoughts from far away. You search out my path and my lying down, and are acquainted with all my ways. Even before a word is on my tongue, O Lord, you know it completely" (Psalm 139:1–4).

Jesus pointed out the outward righteousness of the religious people of His day. Perhaps they acted righteously in public as good examples for others to follow. However, Jesus's religion did not set an example of outward acts as a benchmark for discipleship. The religion and the teachings of Jesus took care of the inward issues before they reflected outward. The righteousness of God must be experienced within the inner being and then manifested into the outer world as love and gratitude. The result of such a relationship is not any propaganda of good works, but the very nature of a child of God.

On this day, check the emotions and motives of your heart. Who are you trying to impress? Are you seeking the presence of the Holy Spirit to funnel your thoughts and be reconciled with the Spirit of God, or are you seeking the praise of people?

PRAYER:
Loving God, You know me well. Not a thought in my mind is hidden from You. Please forgive my every attitude born of selfish ambition, I pray. Help me, dear Lord, that I will seek Your righteousness and holiness in my inner being and not seek human praise. Amen.

Seek the presence of God in your heart and follow the path of personal integrity and holiness.

Believe today you will be salt of the earth and light of the world.

DAY THIRTY-SIX

Then Jesus was led up by the Spirit into the wilderness
to be tempted by the devil.
MATTHEW 4:1

The Spirit of God led Jesus into the wilderness to be tempted. Why did God's Spirit do this? God's Spirit already confirmed that Jesus is the "well-pleasing Son" (Matthew 3:17). Should not the well-pleasing Son go out and serve God? Before Jesus went into public ministry, He was led to identify and articulate His purpose of life. So many times, people, in their zeal, go out to serve God, fail, and then return with hearts full of bitterness and anger. We all must recognize our purpose in life before we enter the field of service.

Jesus's experience in the desert was His school of discipline. The word "temptation" means "to divide." Jesus was divided, pulled between God's purpose and the devil's purpose. The devil sought to divert Jesus from God's purpose. In Jesus's temptations, He allowed the power of God's Spirit to subdue the power of the devil. At the end of such hard schooling, Jesus was tested with subtle tests. They did not appear to be devilish or not fulfilling to God's purpose. Rather, they appeared attractive, as God's will. Jesus's tests were not to kill, commit adultery, or disobey God.

The first test was, "If you are the Son of God, tell these stones to become loaves of bread" (Matthew 4:3). This sounded like a good idea because Jesus was hungry; He had not eaten for forty days. Was it wrong to use God's power to meet His own need? Shouldn't the Son of God use God's power to meet the physical needs of the people, especially to relieve the hunger of the poor?

The devil sought to divide Jesus's mind and have Him follow the devil's direction. However, Jesus sought the heart of God. Both the devil and Jesus used the Word of God as the solution to these tests. The devil took the Word of God literally, whereas Jesus understood the Spirit of the Word. That is the key to understanding God's will. Jesus allowed the inner triangle—the unity of the Spirit—to guide His thoughts for the correct use of God's Word and so defeated the devil's scheme.

PRAYER:
Loving God, help me to understand Your Word, the Spirit of the written Word. Help me to follow Your will and purpose for my life. Amen.

When a thought passes through your mind, filter it through the Spirit of God to discern who prompted such a thought.

Believe today you will be salt of the earth and light of the world.

DAY THIRTY-SEVEN

He fasted forty days and forty nights, and afterwards he was famished.
MATTHEW 4:2

Jesus fasted in the wilderness to seek the will of God and the purpose of His life. The devil used Jesus's physical hunger to try to motivate Him with a quick fix. In seeking God's heart, Jesus not only overcame the devil's scheme but also understood God's purpose for His life. Jesus found His purpose in God's Word—in the Scripture from the book of Isaiah—and accepted it as His mission and purpose for life. Isaiah chapter 61 reads: "The spirit of the Lord God is upon me, because the Lord has anointed me; he has sent me to bring good news to the oppressed, to bind up the brokenhearted, to proclaim liberty to the captives, and release to the prisoners; to proclaim the year of the Lord's favor" (Isaiah 61:1–2).

Considering these verses regarding Jesus's purpose, can you write your purpose statement? Is there a scripture you can identify as your mission statement? Perhaps you say, "My purpose in life is to be a teacher of [fill in with a vocation]." However, the purpose for our lives is greater than our vocations. Would you say, "I want to be a good Christian and go to heaven"? Is that a purpose? Being a good Christian is being obedient to the Spirit of God, isn't it?

What should you do to be obedient to Christ's teachings? The list could be quite long. Take your list to the presence of God, submit your vocational goal and other goals, and seek God's guidance. Believe in your inner being that the Lord can help you reach your goals and fulfill your potential. Then, let go of all worries, for they are negative emotions, and follow the path of love with full submission to the Spirit of God. Whatever you do, do it with enthusiasm. Draw energy from the inner triangle of God, so the outer triangles may live in harmony with God's Spirit.

PRAYER:
Lord, open my understanding so that I may know Your will for my life. Help me to understand Your purpose for me, just as you revealed it to Jesus. Help me, Lord, I pray in Jesus's name. Amen.

Take time to filter your thoughts through the Spirit of God. Visualize serving God's purpose in whatever you do. Write down your mission statement and follow through with it.

Believe today you will be salt of the earth and light of the world.

DAY THIRTY-EIGHT

As the Father has loved me, so I have loved you; abide in my love.
If you keep my commandments, you will abide in my love, just as
I have kept my Father's commandments and abide in his love.
JOHN 15:9–10

Jesus of Nazareth was human, with all the human triangles and their members. He submitted them all to God's love and experienced oneness with the heavenly Father. Jesus's request to His disciples was that just as He remained in God's love, they should remain in His love to fulfill God's purpose.

Love is a positive and productive spiritual force that gives energy to our inner beings. When the love of God permeates our triangles and all the angles come together in harmony, we experience the presence of God within. This is being connected with God, abiding in the Spirit of God. It is having the divine electricity within. Such experience energizes us for action in all situations of life. It gives the assurance—regardless of our vocations—that we are fulfilling the will of God, doing our tasks as to the Lord.

When the love of God controls our lives, we do not seek to set our self-will against God's will. Instead, our fulfillment of life comes from doing the will of God. This changes our attitudes toward life and work. We may do the same work and have the same professions, but our attitudes reflect a great change. Our work attitudes change from merely making a living to serving God in whatever we do.

When we connect with the Spirit of God and abiding in His love, we overcome the negative emotions that limit our potential and possibilities. We are open to God's guidance for vocational change, lifestyle change, and other changes that will help us to be productive servants of God.

PRAYER:
Loving God, help me to abide in Your love and enjoy Your presence. Give me clarity of vision that I will understand Your purpose for my life. Help me to follow Your will in all things. Amen.

Visualize that you are following the will of God as your purpose of life.

Believe today you will be salt of the earth and light of the world.

DAY THIRTY-NINE

Then he poured water into a basin and began to wash the disciples' feet
and to wipe them with the towel that was tied around him.

JOHN 13:5

In Jesus's day, it was customary for Galileans to wash their feet before any meal. The Passover meal was the most important, which Jewish people observed once a year. None of the disciples were willing to do the menial service of washing the others' feet. It was not the observance of the custom that concerned Jesus, but the sullenness and competition He saw in His disciples. It broke His heart, so He got up, took the water and a towel, and washed their feet.

Peter was extremely uncomfortable with Jesus's initiative since foot washing was usually assigned to the host or a servant of the house. He felt shame for allowing his Teacher and Master to wash his feet. However, Peter did not want to wash his fellow disciples' feet. His emotion kept him feeling superior over the other disciples. Such negative emotion paralyzed him from following the teachings of his Master.

This reveals a truth about Christian discipleship. As Christians, we like to serve the Lord. However, our negative, sometimes harsh, attitudes toward those we do not like or those who are different from us keep us from serving them. When we are not willing to serve others, we are controlled by our emotions and not by the Spirit of God.

In sullen silence they all sat with pride.
In humble Spirit the Master stooped down.
With gentle touch, He washed their feet.
Peter, John, and Judas were at the table!

Look at Jesus, my soul, and see the power of love.
Look at Jesus, my soul, and see the power of service.
Are there not any dirty feet for you to wash today?
Are not any water and towels waiting for you?

PRAYER:
Dear Lord, give me a humble heart and fill me with love so that I will stoop down and serve others. Open my eyes so that I will serve You in serving the brothers and sisters in my world. Amen.

Visualize serving others. Look for opportunities to do good and to bless those who are the least deserving.

Believe today you will be salt of the earth and light of the world.

DAY FORTY

Little children, you are from God, and have conquered them;
for the one who is in you is greater than the one who is in the world.
1 JOHN 4:4

"Fear not, for I am with you" is the good news of our Savior (Isaiah 41:10, NKJV). When we face problems, anxieties, and other negative forces, we must affirm God's great power within us. This is the power from the innermost triangle made of the Father, Son, and Holy Spirit. The Apostle John, who faced many difficulties while following the will and purpose of his Lord and Master, experienced this power. He gave control to the indwelling power of the inner triangle and experienced a power of love greater than the power of hate, a power of faith greater than the power of fear, a power of light greater than the power of darkness, and a power of God's presence greater than the loneliness of his exile.

We are creatures of God and a part of nature. We are created to be God's stewards in the natural world. We are interdependent on nature. We breathe air because without it we cannot survive. We eat food, which comes from the natural world. When we take time to understand the workings of our Creator, the earth, and all that is in it, we are humbled and give thanks to God. We will not pollute our environment; we will seek to keep it clean. We will use the resources within it and not abuse them. We will not worship nature, but we will respect it and preserve it as it is God's creation. We will not worry about tomorrow; we will believe that God will provide for all our needs each day. We will enjoy living as children of God, conquering all kinds of fears, for we know "the one who is in us is greater than the one who is in the world" (1 John 4:4).

Today, affirm your relationship with the Creator and give thanks to God. Our bodies are made of material from the earth. God made us stewards of the earth. Let us pick up a few pieces of trash and keep it clean. Let us look at the trees and flowers and praise God. Let us drink a glass of water and quench our thirst. Let us live as God's precious children, full of joyful life and giving thanks to God each and every day.

PRAYER:
Lord, I love You for creating a beautiful world of many things. Lord, I thank You for making me part of it. Help me to sense Your presence by keeping Your world clean. Help me to enjoy life by giving control of my inner being to You today and every day. Amen.

Visualize walking with God in His garden each and every day.

Believe today you will be salt of the earth and light of the world.

GLOSSARY

Belief
a. To accept something as true, genuine, or real
b. The invisible, inner ability of the human spirit to project the possibilities beyond the scope of reason
c. The transcendence and interaction of the human spirit with the Spirit of God, the Creator, to experience God's possibilities beyond human impossibilities

Carnal man
a. Human—male or female—controlled by sensual desires
b. Seeking fulfillment of natural desires and striving for that fulfillment
c. Living with socially-accepted moral values but not submitting to spiritual values
d. Everybody does it, so I do it too.

Faith
a. "Now faith is confidence in what we hope for and assurance about what we do not see" (Hebrews 11:1, NIV).
b. Having confidence in the outcome of an unseen reality
c. Believing in God beyond the impossibilities of the rational mind for positive results
d. Placing confidence in the creative energy of God for positive action

God
a. The source of all things visible and invisible
b. Self-existing and invisible energy
c. Creator, creative energy
d. Love and divine love
e. Father, Heavenly Father, and Eternal Spirit
f. Father, Son, and Holy Spirit
g. The essence of all that is good, wholesome, undefiled, and eternal
h. Eternal light, true light, and light that shines in the darkness

Heart of God
a. Essence of God
b. Loving nature of God

Heart of man
a. The inner nature of man or woman
b. The dwelling place of all members of the four triangles within the physical body
c. The transcendental ability of the human spirit

Human being
a. Man and woman
b. Created being
c. Earthly creature
d. Children of flesh and blood

Inner Being
a. The essence of a person
b. The eleven working members of the human triangles that dwell in the physical body of a living person
c. The seat of all intelligence

Mind
a. The storehouse of all information
b. The control and command center of human intelligence

Old nature
a. The natural tendencies of a human being
b. Unconverted nature
c. When the human triangles act without the influence of God's Spirit

Online with God
a. Experiencing the presence of God
b. Experiencing oneness with the Spirit of God
c. When all members of the human inner being work in harmony with the Spirit of God

New nature
a. The spiritual nature of a human being
b. Converted by the Spirit of Christ to live in harmony with God's Spirit
c. When the human triangles are guided by the Spirit of God

Prayer
a. Earnest quest of the inner being
b. Seeking God's strength and guidance
c. Communing with God
d. When the human spirit reaches out to the divine Spirit and aligns their triangles with the divine triangle

Satan
a. The essence of ungodliness, bad, and evil
b. An invisible force of darkness
c. A destructive force that seeks to destroy life and everything that is good
d. The father of lies and prompter of evil
e. An agent of temptation and destroyer of holiness

Sin
a. "Missing the mark"
b. Deviation from truth
c. A broken relationship
d. Estrangement from God or fellow man
e. Transgression against God's will

Spirit of God
a. The creative energy of the transcending power of God
b. The guidance of God upon a person
c. The active presence of God in a person

Spirit of man
a. The essence of the human inner being that has the discerning power
b. The total sum of the human inner being
c. One part of a triangle in the inner being

Spiritual man
a. A person converted from the natural control of the mind to godly submission
b. The inner being of a person controlled by the Spirit of God

Notes

1. *World Book Encyclopedia*, "Human Body," 1st ed, vol. 9 (Chicago: World Book-Childcraft International, Inc., 1979), 380.

2. Paul Brand and Philip Yancy, *Fearfully and Wonderfully Made* (Grand Rapids: Zondervan Publishing House, 1980), 26.

3. George A. Buttrick, et al., ed., *The Interpreter's Dictionary of the Bible*, vol. 4 (Nashville: Abingdon-Cokesbury Press, 1962), 428.

4. Kevin T. Favero, *The Science of the Soul: Scientific Evidence of Human Souls* (St. Paul, MN: Beaver's Pond Press Inc., 2004).

5. Wikipedia, "Human spirit," last modified December 17, 2020, https://en.wikipedia.org/wiki/Human_spirit.

6. *World Book Encyclopedia*, "Reason," 1st ed., vol. 16. (Chicago: World Book-Childcraft International, Inc., 1979), 163.

7. David B. Guralnik, ed., *Webster's New World Dictionary*, "Emotion," vol. 1, 2nd ed. (Cleveland, OH: The World Publishing Company, 1970).

8. *World Book Encyclopedia*, "Thought and Judgement," 1st ed., vol. 19 (Chicago: World Book-Childcraft International, Inc., 1979), 206.

9. Robert Maynard Hutchins, ed., *Great Books of the Western World*, vol. 35 (Chicago: William Benton, Encyclopedia Britannica, Inc. 1952), 179.

10. *World Book Encyclopedia*, "Mind: Physical and Mental Relationship," 1st ed., vol. 13 (Chicago: World Book-Childcraft International, Inc., 1979), 475.

11. The Work of Manfred Davidmann, www.solhamm.org.

12. *World Book Encyclopedia*, "Theories," 1st ed., vol. 7 (Chicago: World Book-Childcraft International, Inc., 1979), 456.

13. John J. Ratey and Eric Hagerman, *Spark: The Revolutionary New Science of Exercise and the Brain* (New York: Little, Brown and Company, 2008), 41.

14. *World Book Encyclopedia*, "Freud," 1st ed., (Chicago: World Book-Childcraft International, Inc., 1979).

15. *The Interpreter's Bible Vol. 1*, 1st ed., (Nashville: Abingdon Press, 1952), 482.

16. Daniel B. Merrick, ed., "Nicene Creed," Chalice Hymnal (St. Louis, MO: Chalice Press, 1995).

17. David B. Guralnik, ed., *Webster's New World Dictionary* vol. 1, 2nd ed. (Cleveland, OH: The World Publishing Company, 1970).

18. Source unknown.

19. Erik H. Erikson, *Identity: Youth and Crisis* (New York: W. W. Norton & Company, 1994), 71.

20. Larry Stein, Monte Nesbitt, and Jim Kamas, "Texas Fruit and Nut Production: Persimmons - Wild Varieties," Agrilifeextension, tamu.edu, https://agrilifeextension.tamu.edu/library/farming/texas-fruit-and-nut-production-persimmons/.

21. George A. Buttrick, et al., ed., *The Interpreter's Dictionary of the Bible*, vol. 11 (Nashville: Abingdon-Cokesbury Press, 1962), 718.

22. Robert Maynard Hutchins, ed., *Great Books of the Western World*, vol. 3 (Chicago: William Benton, Encyclopedia Britannica, Inc., 1952), 593.

23. Frances R. Havergal, "Take My Life and Let It Be," Public Domain. https://hymnary.org/text/take_my_life_and_let_it_be.

BIBLIOGRAPHY

Adler, Mortimer J. *The Great Ideas, A Syntopicon of Great Book of the Western World. Vol. 2.* Chicago, Illinois: Encyclopedia Britannica, Inc. 1952.

Anthony, Robert. *Total Self-Confidence.* San Diego, California: New Thought Publications. 1979.

Bradberry, Travis, and Jean Graves. *Emotional intelligence.* San Diego, California: Talent Smart, Inc. 2009.

Brand, Paul Wilson, and Philip Yancy. *Fearfully and Wonderfully Made.* Grand Rapids, Michigan: Zondervan Publishing House. 1980.

Buttrick, George A. *The Interpreter's Bible.* Nashville, Tennessee: Abingdon Press. 1962.

Buttrick, George A. *The Interpreter's Dictionary of the Bible.* Nashville, Tennessee: Abingdon Press. 1962.

Davidmann, Manfred. The work of Manfred Davidmann. www.solhamm.org.

Erikson, Erik H. *Identity Youth and Crisis.* New York, New York: W. W. Norton & Company. 1968.

Favero, Kevin T. *The Science of the Soul: Scientific Evidence of Human Souls.* St. Paul, Minnesota: Beaver's Pond Press Inc. 2004.

Freud, Sigmund. 1856–1939. *Theories,* Ed. World Book Encyclopedia. Vol. 7. Chicago, Illinois: World Book-Childcraft International, Inc. 1979.

Goodrick, Edward W., and John R. Kohlenberger III. *The Complete Concordance to the New International Version.* Grand Rapids, Michigan: Zondervan Publishing House. 1981.

Helminiak, Daniel A. Wikipedia. *Human spirit.*

Locke, John. 1632–1704. *An Essay, concerning Human Understanding.* Great Books of the Western World. Robert Maynard Hutchins, ed.,

Chicago, Illinois: William Benton, Encyclopedia Britannica Inc. 1952. Vol. 3. 593.

Marshall Pickering Communications. *Vine's Expository Dictionary of New Testament Words.* London, England: Evangelical Christian Publisher's Association. 1952.

Merrick, Daniel B., ed. *Chalice Hymnal.* St. Louis, Missouri: Chalice Press. 1995.

O'Conner, Elizabeth. *Our Many Selves.* New York, New York: Harper & Row, Publishers, Inc. 1971.

Peale, Norman Vincent, and Ruth Stafford. *Discovering The Power of Positive Thinking.* Pawling, New York: Peale Center for Christian Living. January 2000.

Peale, Norman Vincent. *The Positive Power of Jesus Christ.* Wheaton, Illinois: Tyndale House Publishers, Inc. 1980.

Peale, Norman Vincent. *How to Be Your Best: A Treasury of Practical Ideas.* Pawling, New York: Foundation for Christian Living. 1990.

Prabhupada, Bhaktivedanta Swami. *Bhagavad-Gita.* Abridged Edition. New York, New York: Bhaktivenda Book Trust Printing. 1968.

Ratey, John J., MD, and Eric Hagerman. *The Revolutionary New Science of Exercise and the Brain.* New York, New York: Little, Brown and Company. 2008.

Stein, Larry, Monte Nesbitt, and Jim Kamas. Extension Fruit Specialist. The Texas A&M System.

Webster's New World Dictionary, 2nd. College Edition. New York, New York: The World Publishing Company. 1970.

World Book Encyclopedia. Chicago, Illinois: World Book-Childcraft International, Inc. 1979.

ABOUT THE AUTHOR

Dr. C. Philip Chacko retired from the Christian ministry after forty-four years of serving churches in Texas. He authored worship materials used internationally in alignment with the liturgical calendar, including the *Love on the Cross*, *Forty Days with Jesus*, *Women of the Cross*, and *Fifty Days to Power* programs.

Philip was raised in Kerala, a state along the southwestern coast of India, where rich orthodox traditions were first instilled by the disciple Thomas in AD 52. After graduating from Southern Asia Bible College in Bangalore, India, he came to the United States to study further at Oral Roberts University in Tulsa, Oklahoma, and at Brite Divinity School in Fort Worth, Texas. At Texas Christian University, he earned his Master of Divinity and Doctor of Ministry degrees. After more than twenty-two years as a pastor of Disciples of Christ churches, Philip became the area minister for the Northeast region of Texas and served sixty-four congregations until 2006. He returned to pastoral ministry before retiring in 2019. He has three adult children and three grandchildren. He enjoys writing and gardening with his wife, Elizabeth, in Tyler, Texas.